DISCIPLINE BY NEGOTIATION

DISCIPLINE
by NEGOTIATION

Methods for Managing
Student Behavior

DANIEL R. TOMAL, Ph.D.

Concordia University

TECHNOMIC
PUBLISHING CO., INC.
LANCASTER · BASEL

Discipline by Negotiation
a TECHNOMIC publication

Technomic Publishing Company, Inc.
851 New Holland Avenue, Box 3535
Lancaster, Pennsylvania 17604 U.S.A.

Printed in the United States of America
10   9   8   7   6   5   4   3   2   1

Main entry under title:
    Discipline by Negotiation: Methods for Managing Student Behavior

A Technomic Publishing Company book
Bibliography: p. 147
Includes index p. 155

Library of Congress Catalog Card No. 98-85446
ISBN No. 1-56676-673-7

CONTENTS

Appendix C: National Association of Secondary School Principals Weapons in Schools Position Statement

Appendix D: Teacher Discipline Style Inventory

Appendix E: Student Disciplinary Offenses Assessment

Appendix F: Teacher Class Management Survey

Bibliography

Index

About The Author

DISCIPLINE CONTINUES TO be a significant problem for our schools. Aggression, harassment, defiance, fighting, classroom disruption, and violence are but a few of the disciplinary problems teachers face. Throughout the country, teachers are utilizing a variety of approaches and creative schemes for managing school discipline with varying degrees of success. Yet, even with these many approaches, teachers continue to constantly search for more effective means of handling discipline.

How can teachers reduce disciplinary problems? What are methods to improve student motivation? What are the most effective ways of teaching difficult students? How can educators successfully change a poor or mediocre school and turn it into a model of excellence? These are just a few of the questions that form the underlying basis of this book.

This book has been written based upon years of study, research, and inservice training workshops on the topic of discipline. The principles have been tested on the firing line in both public and private elementary and secondary schools and in university classrooms. The book includes many tried and proven principles and ideas from teachers and administrators. *Discipline by Negotiation* is based upon a collaborative approach of recognizing the needs of students and teachers in maintaining order and achieving the best learning environment in the school.

The principles of Discipline by Negotiation can be used to support any disciplinary school program. It is a practical and no-nonsense approach that can be used by any educator—early childhood, elementary, secondary, or the university level. Negotiation by discipline gives flexibility to "zero tolerance" policies and provides a practical strategy for teachers to deal with discipline in their classrooms on a day-to-day basis. It is a viable model that can be used for restoring and maintaining sanity and safety to schools.

FEATURES OF THE BOOK

The most intriguing and unique feature of this book, unlike any other book written on discipline, is the introduction of clearly defined student negotiating tactics and teacher countertactics used in student–teacher disciplinary situations. Understanding these student tactics and developing effective skills in applying the countertactics can significantly improve any educator's managing of disciplinary problems. The principles of discipline by negotiation can also assist educators in motivating students, managing the most difficult students, and building any schoool into an outstanding educational institution.

Another valuable feature is the numerous examples of methods of managing offensive and violent students. Real-life disciplinary situations are presented that contain actual vignettes with practical and "street-wise" solutions that any educator can utilize in resolving disciplinary problems.

A unique feature that has been appreciated by teachers during inservice teacher training workshops is the specific negotiating countertactics that teachers can utilize in dealing with the numerous student tactics they see from students on a daily basis. These countertactics are presented in an effective and straightforward manner based upon the most commonly used tactics used by students today.

Several other features of this book include the following:

- Step-by-step procedures for counseling and disciplining students are presented for use in any disciplinary situation.
- A review of the major discipline theories and models by some of leading researchers and educators is given.
- A comprehensive description of the common causes of misbehavior and associated student defense mechanisms is presented as a foundational framework in stimulating thought and understanding.
- Up-to-date guidelines on school policies, federal and case laws, and regulations affecting disciplining of students and maintaining safety within schools are given.
- Practical tips and strategies develop skills in managing student gang and criminal activities.
- A detailed explanation of the rights and responsibilities of students, teachers, and administrators is outlined.

The principles of discipline by negotiation have been applied in schools with a myriad of problems. For example, one large Chicago-area school was experiencing low teacher morale, ineffective leadership, high rates of student disciplinary incidents, excessive absenteeism, and mediocre student test performance. The principles of Discipline by Negotiation were implemented as a process to diagnose the organizational problems and to develop and implement specific action plans that helped turn the school around.

Other schools that have implemented principles from this book have ranged from teachers and administrators who desired to improve their handling of disciplinary problems, decrease student absenteeism, improve student motivation, and increase teacher morale, to enhancing overall student performance and the school environment. The principles of Discipline by Negotiation have also been taught in undergraduate and graduate classes.

REFERENCE AIDS

The book contains a rich source of educational and reference aids that can be used by educators in applying the principles of Discipline by Negotiation. Some of these aids include

- developing a school uniform discipline policy
- implementing a progressive discipline program
- diagnosing an organization and making meaningful educational improvements
- establishing a successful peer mediation program
- understanding and utilizing teacher discipline styles through an inventory assessment
- identifying student disciplinary offenses and establishing uniform action for misconduct through assessment and class management instruments

ORGANIZATION OF THE BOOK

The book has been written for an educator to first understand the basis for student misbehavior, organizational effects that impact student behavior, principles and strategies for reaching agreement, negotiating tactics and countertactics, and how to create a win-win organization. Each chapter builds upon the others. Several illustrations are also provided to give a visual representation of the information to help the reader understand the material.

Given that the material in this book has been developed and refined throughout the years through research and teacher inservice workshops,

MANY PEOPLE PROVIDED support and input in preparing this book. I especially appreciate my wife, Annette, for editing the manuscript, and Pam Chrusciel, for typing it. Many teachers have attended my workshops on this topic and have given me feedback, case situations, and support. I appreciate many school districts where I have given seminars, such as Chicago Public Schools, Proviso Township High Schools, Park Forest School District 163, West Chicago District 33, Bellwood School District 88, Cicero School District 99, Lake Central School Corporation, Michigan City Township High Schools, Findlay Schools, Concordia University, and Lutheran Church Missouri Synod schools. Lastly, I would like to extend my gratitude to the people who endorsed this book and gave me insight for this project.

I VIVIDLY REMEMBER my first day of teaching. I had just completed all my coursework at Ball State University and was student teaching at a middle school in Muncie, Indiana. I had eagerly prepared a lesson plan and hardly slept a wink in anticipation of my first lesson to a seventh-grade class. As I awaited the start of class, I watched the rambunctious group of students talking and running about. When the bell rang, I asked everyone to sit down so we could begin the lesson. And then, much to my surprise, nothing happened! They completely ignored me as I stood there staring at my lesson plan. I felt dumbfounded, and I didn't know what to do, so I desperately tried everything from pleading to threatening them to get them to sit down and be quiet.

I realized at that moment that I was experiencing my very first discipline problem. Fortunately, my student teacher supervisor intervened and gracefully settled the group down and gained their attention. As I reflected on this situation, I concluded that even though I had taken many teaching preparation courses, I had never been trained how to get the students to sit down and pay attention.

Somehow, I have the feeling, as I think about this frustrating experience, that all beginning teachers can relate to this situation. I must admit that, being a persistent individual, I was determined that a group of little seventh graders was not going to get the best of me. I soon learned that being a good teacher meant being competent in handling discipline problems and that it required a combination of patience, skill, and a cast-iron stomach.

Discipline is an art, and all teachers must develop skill in handling student disciplinary problems. Whether a teacher must gain the attention of students or deal with violence, teachers need to be able to establish a classroom environment that ensures good behavior and learning.

My next dose of discipline came when I received my first permanent full-time teaching position at a large inner-city high school near Chicago.

If I thought trying to get a group of seventh graders to be quiet and take a seat was difficult, I was really in for a surprise. During this first week, I witnessed everything from a student putting hydrochloric acid into a science teacher's coffee cup and personal threats by students against fellow teachers to drugs, gang activity, and violence.

I remember during this first week walking down the school hallway while classes were in session and meeting a group of thug-like students walking toward me. As I approached them, I kindly asked them where they were going and if they had a hall pass. They proceeded to taunt me as I asked them to go to their class. They finally stopped and walked out of the building ignoring me. While I knew students were not to be in the hallway during classes, I felt ineffective in actually gaining control of the situation. I must admit, I also felt rather intimidated, embarrassed, and slightly scared given that these students appeared to be only a couple of years younger than myself. Not knowing what to do, I went to the school disciplinary dean and explained the incident and asked him for advice. He proceeded to explain to me various passages from the school policy handbook and then concluded by indicating that the students shouldn't be in the hallway and that next time I should ask them for their identification cards.

Two days later, I found myself in the very same situation with the same students and proceeded to follow the advice of the disciplinary dean. This time I sternly requested their identification cards, which evoked a hysterical response of laughter. They not only walked away from me, but one of them flipped me a profane gesture. I remember feeling totally humiliated and angered. Thankfully, it was Friday, and I had the weekend to reflect on the situation. As I thought about the incident over the weekend, I soon realized that there wasn't any discipline "cookbook" that could give all the answers in helping teachers deal with disciplinary situations. However, it seemed that some teachers were inherently able to handle disciplinary problems more effectively than others. I also realized that teachers couldn't send all their disciplinary problems to the disciplinary dean, and that the job of teachers was handling their own disciplinary problems. I realized in this situation, if I were going to be successful as a teacher, I had to figure out how to handle this situation by myself.

It was at that point that I realized that dealing with student disciplinary problems is similar to dealing with other interactions with people. I concluded that the same sense of "street smarts" I had used in surviving and growing up as a teenager could also be applied in dealing with student disciplinary problems. Essentially, I realized that every interaction with students involved a negotiating element, whereby both parties wanted something. The key, I realized, was to obtain a meaningful settlement that was in the best interests of the school. I ended the weekend by deciding to rely upon these "street smarts" in dealing with student discipline problems.

I started out my second week by once again encountering these same students in the hallway. Being convinced that these students were simply messing around and not in class where they were supposed to be, I once again confronted them. As they started to taunt me, this time I resorted to my "street smarts." With my eyes piercing through them, I threw my books down on the floor and began loudly demanding "I don't want to hear anymore crap out of you and get to your class immediately!" At that instant, I recalled the students looking at me as if I had gone crazy. In fact, one of the students replied, "Come on, guys, let's get to class; I think this teacher means business, and we don't want to screw with him." I watched as the students went directly to study hall and sat down in their seats without a word.

Now I'm not suggesting or advocating the use of hysterics or hostile teacher behavior in every situation. However, in this particular situation, it worked. I realized that my showing of strength in how a teacher handled himself had a huge impact on the effectiveness in a given situation. I imagine that many experienced teachers have resorted to this similar assertive behavior in handling a difficult situation. I also recognized that every situation requires a different disciplinary style. It may be appropriate to be very sensitive and caring in one situation; and in another situation, assertiveness may be appropriate. Therefore, it is the purpose of this book to help beginning and seasoned teachers to develop effective negotiating skills to become more "street wise" in handling disciplinary problems in their classrooms.

I believe that all disciplinary situations with students involve interactions that contain an element of negotiation. Negotiations can be applied to any student behavior such as open defiance, apathy, hostility, chronic talking, horseplay, harassment, and insubordination. Negotiation involves the process of two parties working with each other to arrive at a settlement. Often, students desire to obtain something that is inappropriate, and the teacher wants to correct the behavior. For example, a student may desire to disrupt the class by talking without permission in an attempt to gain attention, and a teacher desires the student to be attentive and resourceful in class. The ability to reach a settlement that is in the best interest of the school is the ultimate goal of the teacher.

I'll conclude this introduction by telling one last story. In the summer of 1997, as I was sitting in my study at home preparing for the upcoming school year, I received a telephone call from a person who identified himself as Toby Smith (name has been changed). The person asked me if I remembered him, and I said no. He stated that he had been a student of mine in 1977. He said he had been trying to reach me since 1986 and finally was able to track me down using the Internet. I must admit, at this point I was getting a little concerned as to why he would be so determined to locate me after so many years. As he spoke, I started to vaguely remember him, even to the point of remembering the actual place he used to sit. He explained to me that he had discovered I had moved several times and that he was happy he had finally located me. He commented that he had been somewhat of a troublemaker in school and that while in school he had planned on becoming a TV repairman. At this point, I started wondering exactly where this conversation was leading.

Eventually, he indicated that the purpose of his call was to thank me for something that had occurred while he was a student in my classroom. Toby stated that one day while he was in my class, I took him to the side and told him that he was "special." He said I told him that he was a person with exceptional talents and that I believed he could achieve much greater heights and become an electronic engineer. Toby went on to say that he had become a senior electronic engineer in a major electronic corporation and the director of the entire division. He indicated that if it had not been for my inspiring words to him that he would never have achieved his career success. He again stated that he was very grateful to me and simply wanted to thank me.

I must admit, once I realized the purpose of this call, I had a great sense of relief and felt deeply touched by his obvious sincerity. And, while I was grateful for his comments, I was most concerned about the many kids I could have negatively influenced or misguided. As teachers, I believe we all strive to receive a telephone call like this one from Toby, which often are few and far between. I believe, as dedicated teachers, receiving a telephone call like this is the ultimate goal of teaching. Much like a physician who heals a patient, or a technician who repairs a computer, our profession is one of a "calling" where we do our best to help students learn and inspire them to achieve their God-given talents. I hope that the principles and techniques of Discipline by Negotiation will help all teachers become more effective in managing disciplinary problems and motivating students to achieve their very best.

CHAPTER 1

Understanding Student Misbehavior

CAUSES OF MISBEHAVIOR

MANAGING DISCIPLINE IS a major problem facing our schools today. The annual Phi Delta Kappa/Gallup Poll of Public's Attitudes Toward the Public Schools has consistently ranked discipline as one of the top problems facing schools. In the 1996 survey, discipline, along with drug abuse, fighting, violence and gang-related issues, was the biggest problem facing local schools (Elam, Rose, & Gallup, 1996).

The need to find the most effective methods and techniques to manage disciplinary problems has been a constant struggle for teachers and administrators. Teachers routinely deal with students who bring into their classrooms a multiple range of dysfunctional behaviors, such as depression, aggression, hostility, resentment, victim mentality, self-image problems, guilt, isolation, blaming disorders, obsessive compulsion, and substance abuse-related problems.

There have been many attempts to create theories and models to try to understand the formulation of human personalities. The theories of Transactional Analysis (TA) have been very useful in helping teachers better understand people's personalities and behaviors (Berne, 1964; Harris, 1967). As an outgrowth of TA, a basic model called the "Life Position Theory" has been developed to provide a foundation for educators in understanding the formulation of human personality and the possible root causes of student misbehavior (see Figure 1.1).

The premise of the Life Position Theory suggests that the development of a student's personality is largely based upon the treatment he/she received as a child. For example, the first personality, the win-win student, refers to the student who has a healthy disposition about school and life. This student feels good about himself/herself and others. This student readily accepts compliments from others and also gives compliments to other people.

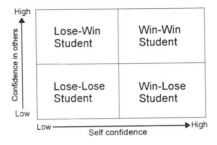

Figure 1.1. Life position model.

The personality of the win-win student was developed as an outgrowth of being raised in a normal and loving home in which he/she received appropriate upbringing and respect from his/her parents. As an infant, this child was given love and nurturance and learned to feel good about himself/herself. The win-win student was conditioned to respect authority and consequently his/her school, teachers, and classmates. The attitude of the win-win student is one of a cooperative spirit in which there is a positive and open desire to have healthy relationships and succeed. The win-win student is generally not a problem in the classroom. This student is motivated and communicates his/her feelings in an acceptable manner. The challenge of the teacher in dealing with win-win students is to continually reinforce their good behavior so these students can remain motivated and perform to their highest potential.

The second personality, the win-lose student, is the person who fundamentally has a life position that he/she is always right and that everyone else is against him/her. The win-lose student is filled with anger and resentment and is very critical about teachers and the school. He/she has high confidence in himself/herself, but feels others do not. The development of this win-lose personality is theorized to be based upon the child's upbringing in a hostile or physical environment. For example, as an infant, the win-lose student might have been physically abused by a father. Given that an infant does not understand the reason for the abuse, the child can only understand how he/she feels as a result of the abuse. This infant develops a position that when his/her father is around him/her, he/she feels bad and hurts because of the physical pain inflicted upon him/her. As a result, the win-lose student develops a personality that indicates that "If I am by myself, I feel good and I must not be the problem, but when others are around me I feel bad and hurt, so others must be bad."

This attitude is reinforced by the win-lose child and develops into a personality position for the rest of his/her life. Typical behavior of the win-lose student in the classroom is based upon an attitude that the school is out to get them and that rules are a form of punishment. The win-lose students are demanding to teachers and enjoy putting others down through their cynical and fault-finding attitude. They often become involved in gangs and violent activities. In severe cases, the win-lose student may ultimately end up in jail.

The win-lose student is constantly causing problems in both the classroom and society. He/she refuses to accept any responsibility for their behavior. The win-lose student can be a very difficult person to manage within the school setting. They harbor a deep-down feeling of low self-esteem but manifest this attitude through seeking power. They often associate with other students who have similar attitudes. The win-lose student may attempt to influence vulnerable students and desire to control them. Even as these win-lose students commit various crimes against the school and society, they constantly seek recognition, and they feel they are right and that others are against them.

The third personality style is the lose-lose student. The lose-lose student is defensive, depressed, stubborn, and has little or no motivation to do anything. As an infant, the lose-lose student might have been a product of an unwanted pregnancy and then abandoned early on as an infant. The lose-lose child might have temporarily lived with various relatives in a variety of homes and never enjoyed permanent residency with a mother and a father. The lose-lose child develops a mentality that life is miserable and empty. The infant feels that when he/she is by himself/herself, he/she is lonely, sad, and has no one who loves him/her. When the lose-lose infant is with others, the reality is that the situation often turns out to be just temporary. The lose-lose infant soon becomes distrusting and loses confidence in the love of others. In essence, the lose-lose child develops a personality that is somewhat based upon a miserable and apathetic position.

The lose-lose student is one who typically sits in a classroom and does nothing and does not care about anything. He/she has little confidence in self or others. This lose-lose student may refuse to do homework, participate in class activities, and has little interest in developing friendships and getting close to other students and teachers. A lose-lose student can be a very difficult student to manage in the classroom given that he/she has such a low self-esteem and is insubordinate. In serious situations, this is the type of student who may participate in self-abuse or commit suicide.

The fourth personality is the lose-win student. This student generally feels good toward others but deep down may feel badly towards himself/herself. The lose-win student lacks self-confidence and feels others are better than himself/herself. As an infant, this child might have received inconsistent love and affection from parents. For example, the child might have been a product of a home where the parents were too busy with other things in their lives to give much attention to the child. The child begins to feel badly towards himself/herself and wonders to himself/herself, "What must I do to obtain unconditional love and reinforcement from my parents?" For example, this student may bring home a report card with good grades, but his/her parents may disregard it or give little positive praise for his/her efforts. This lose-win child develops a mentality that he/she is not as good as others and can never seem to live up to the expectations of his/her parents.

The lose-win child will often compliment others, but may find it difficult to receive compliments. The lose-win student often feels confused, frustrated, and bewildered in the classroom. He/she constantly worries about failing and not achieving the expectations of the teacher. This student may feel that other students are competent, but that he/she lacks the same degree of competence and abilities. While this student often is a person who is hard to motivate and demands constant positive reinforcement, he/she generally is not as difficult to manage as the lose-lose or win-lose student.

The lose-win student, however, can manifest his/her behavior in other ways, such as attempting to oversucceed by attempting to climb the tops of mountains without ever reaching the top. No matter how well the student performs, it can never be good enough. This student may also try very hard to participate in student activities and attempt to become very popular, while underneath possessing feelings of low self-confidence. Underneath the facade, these students are searching to receive the unconditional love from their parents. In extreme situations, these students may become co-dependent upon others and may be easily influenced by peer pressure. These students may also attempt to become overachievers in life and may ultimately become frustrated and never totally satisfied with relationships or their accomplishments.

Understanding the Life Position Theory can be useful in dealing with students' behavior in the classroom. By understanding the life position of a student, the educator can have insight into the reasons for students' behavior. For example, in dealing with the win-lose student, a teacher may find it important to be very stern and assertive. The win-lose student may often become demanding and cynical and attempt to blame others for his/her behavior. The teacher needs to understand that this win-lose student needs to develop responsibility for his/her behavior and the teacher should not tolerate the student's attempts to blame others.

The lose-lose student can be a very difficult person to manage in the classroom. Many times these students may sit in the classroom and do nothing and the teacher may be inclined to ignore him/her. This student will need a constant high degree of encouragement and reinforcement as a person. It is important for the teacher to allow the lose-lose student to feel like a part of the class and to develop a sense of security. However, the teacher should be careful not to reinforce the lose-lose attitude. These students may state that they are incapable of performing certain learning activities, and the teacher must be careful not to reinforce this victim-type mentality.

The lose-win student is a person who needs a high degree of self-confidence building. The teacher will need to reinforce positive behavior on a consistent basis. Peer identification is important to these students, as well as the building of this student's self-esteem.

The formation of a student's personality is dependent upon his/her self-concept. All students live in a multi-dimensional environment, whereby they learn to understand about themselves and others around them given their situation. As far back as 400 B.C., Socrates developed a basic life premise, "Know thyself." A student's perception of himself/herself has a major impact on the child's behavior in the classroom.

Students receive a variety of cues and personal messages from their peers and teachers which reinforce attitudes and behaviors. If students are heavily influenced by "the ideal self-concept," they will often embark in classroom behaviors that reinforce this image. For example, if students view themselves as powerful and influential, they will tend to dominate discussion and seek power and control in the classroom. In reality, the student's self-concept can be a basis of creating their personal paradigm in how he/she views his/her school environment and the world.

Peer perceptions of a student help to shape a student's attitude and behavior in the classroom. For example, if peers' perceptions of a student are ones of strong leadership, their impressions may create a self-fulfilling prophecy and the student will become a leader. In essence, the views of the peers become a reality in the mind of the student. Likewise, a student's own self-concept plays an important part in shaping his/her own behavior. For example, a student who has a strong religious foundation and believes that he/she is a righteous individual, may be less impacted by negative peer influence and demonstrate good behavior. Therefore, the importance of developing a positive self-concept in students is critical in establishing order and good behavior in the classroom.

Other factors that contribute to students having discipline problems in the classroom include the nature of the students' home environments, societal influences, the students' personalities, and the school itself. Factors within the student's home, regardless of the student's socioeconomic level, that can cause a student to misbehave are:

(*1*) Highly dysfunctional or stressful home environment
(*2*) Overly strict or lenient parenting
(*3*) Lack of parental guidance within the home
(*4*) Lack of consistency in administering discipline within the home
(*5*) Lack of interest by parents regarding student's behavior and performance in the school
(*6*) Physical abuse of children by parents within the home
(*7*) Psychological abuse of children by parents
(*8*) Poor relationships among family members within the home
(*9*) Negative peer relationships and influences within the home

Many of the same behaviors that are conditioned by the home environment continue on into the classroom. If students have dysfunctional influences within their home environments, these same tendencies may exist within the classroom too. Societal variables can also impact upon the student's behavior. Students who are exposed to violent and aggressive behavior through the media (e.g., television and radio) may have a tendency to demonstrate these behaviors in the classroom. There tends to be a relationship between the amount of violence students are exposed to through the media and their own aggressive behavior in the classroom.

The school itself can contribute to the overall behavior of students. Schools that have characteristics of being overcrowded, difficult to manage, poor leadership, negative attitudes and low morale among teachers, poor environmental conditions, and overall poor scheduling can contribute to students' misbehaviors.

VALUES, CHARACTER, AND INTERPERSONAL RELATIONS

Another variable that influences a student's attitude and behavior in the classroom is the student's personal value system. A person's values are determined by such factors as the person's geographical area, religion, school, economic status, media, and peer group. Typical values include morality, power, loyalty, sense of justice, honesty and trust, and need for achievement. The formation of a student's value system is determined at a very early age. There are three stages of a person's value system: imprinting, modelling, and socialization.

The imprinting stage begins when the student is an infant. During this stage, the child mimics the behaviors of those around him/her. For example, when a parent smiles, the infant learns to smile back. These learned behaviors are reinforced as the infant develops.

The second stage, modelling, begins around the age of eight and ends during the early teenage years. During modelling, students develop role models with which they identify and they adopt similar attitudes and behaviors. Students at this stage often begin to copy and adopt the styles of media personalities and celebrities.

Socialization, the third stage, involves the development of a student's value system based upon his/her interaction with other students. This stage is formed throughout the teenage years. The idea of the "significant other" becomes a powerful influence in how well students behave in the classroom.

The importance of students socializing with peers who have good values is critical in the socialization stage. Students who develop a value system built upon honesty, trust, and morality may be more prone to respect the classroom teacher and the rules and regulations of the school. Those students concerned with developing power may more interested in controlling others, establishing authority, and influencing other people. Socially unacceptable values that are programmed into students at a very early age and reinforced may be difficult to reshape.

Based upon their value system, the student will place a varying degree of value on school, education, work, and living in society. A student's value system is determined by his/her environment—family, peer group, media, music, the school system, and religion. For example, a student from a lower-class socioeconomic system may view people in authority positions, such as police, teachers, and school officials, as people who are to be avoided and distrusted. On the other hand, a student from a middle-class socioeconomic level might view these same authority figures as a source of security and as people to provide services to them. The lower-class student may have more inherent distrust and display more open defiance to teachers, while middle-class students may have relatively more respect for them. Education may also be viewed as something to endure by lower-class students until they can enter the working world and make money for survival, while middle-class students may view education as a means for achieving success in life. Lower-class students may place less significance on the value of homework and investing in educational resources.

Upper-class students may also view teachers with disrespect if they come from a home environment that does not respect teachers because of their perceived middle-class socioeconomic status within society. This type of attitude might manifest into disciplinary problems within the classroom such as challenging a teacher's opinions about the fairness of classroom rules that are inconsistent with the student's personal view.

A student's value system may affect his/her behavior in unexpected ways. A teacher once told a story about a student who was from a welfare family where the family lacked the basics of adequate food, shelter, and security. In a conversation between the student and teacher, it was determined that the teacher had lost a hubcap on his car and was mentioning the fact that he would need to purchase another one. Hearing this teacher's situation, the student, later that evening, located a car in the school parking lot with the same type of hubcap and stole one of the hubcaps for the teacher. At school the next morning, the student presented the hubcap to the teacher as a gift. When the teacher realized what had happened, he discussed it with the student. The teacher eventually realized that this student placed little value on respecting the property of others and did not understand why this act was wrong. In the student's view (i.e., paradigm), a teacher who he liked needed a hubcap, and he saw nothing wrong in stealing a hubcap from someone else and giving it to his teacher. In essence, the student actually saw the committing of an immoral act as a good deed for the teacher.

It is important for teachers to understand the impact of a student's value system in relationship to classroom behavior. All students are different, and these individual differences are often based upon a student's programmed value system, which will impact how he/she behaves in a school setting. Inservice teacher workshops based upon understanding individual differences, values, and interpersonal relations can significantly help teachers better understand the underlying reasons for student attitudes, character, and behaviors.

STUDENT DEFENSE MECHANISMS

Depending upon a student's personality, he/she will often use a number of different defense mechanisms to justify their misbehavior. Students who do not accept responsibility or accountability for their actions

Defense Mechanism	**Student Behavior**
1. Denial	1. Refuses to accept Behavior
2. Projection	2. Projects feelings in others
3. Reaction Formation	3. States opposite feelings
4. Manic Behavior	4. Acts aggressively in class

Figure 1.2. *Student defense mechanisms.*

will attempt to divert the teacher's attention through various defense strategies. For example, five typical defense mechanisms commonly found in students are (1) denial, (2) projection, (3) reaction formation, (4) manic behavior, and (5) fantasy/idealization (see Figure 1.2).

Denial

Students who utilize the denial defense mechanism will often respond by denying they have a problem. When confronted with a disciplinary problem, these students often respond by lying. They refuse to be held accountable for their actions. For example, if a student is caught talking without permission, the student may respond that he/she was not talking. These students are also persistent and emotional in their denial.

Projection

Projection is a common defense mechanism used by students who not only fail to accept responsibility for their action, but displace blame onto other people. For example, if the student is disorganized, the student may actually blame the teacher for disorganization; or if a student is tired in class and not paying attention, he/she may state that the teacher is actually tired and not paying attention.

The student attempts to project his/her feelings onto the other person in order to compensate for his/her own feelings of inadequacy. Students who use projection can be difficult to manage given their adamant feelings that their behavior is the problem of someone other than themselves.

Reaction Formation

Students who use the reaction formation defense mechanism will do the opposite than what they actually desire. For example, a student may actually say that they dislike school, when in reality, they like school. This opposing statement is a defense mechanism for their inability to internalize their actions and feelings. The student may utilize reaction formation in an attempt to avoid disciplinary action or as justification for behavior.

Manic Behavior

Students who use manic behavior as a defense mechanism demonstrate aggressive behavior as a means to develop power and control. For example, students may misbehave in a pursuit for power and attention from their peers. A typical statement may be, "You can't dictate to me and push me around." They will often refuse to obey classroom rules and teacher requests through their aggressive and hostile behavior.

Fantasy/Idealization

Students who use fantasy/idealization as a defense mechanism are heavily influenced by role models such as sports figures on television or movie actors (i.e., heroes and heroines). They may fantasize about being gang leaders by listening to gangster rap music and videos. As a result, these students may exhibit misbehaviors in order to gain attention and to mimic their heroes and heroines. These students often desire to be center-stage in the classroom. They may constantly distract the teacher and cause havoc. They tend to live out their fantasies in the classroom by idealizing these behaviors.

Teachers who have an understanding of these basic defense mechanisms can be more successful in understanding why students behave the way they do. For example, John was a student who would regularly involve the defense mechanisms of denial and reaction formation at the same time. John would often deny any responsibility for his misbehavior in the classroom and would openly state that he disliked the teacher and school.

During follow-up counseling sessions with John, it became apparent that this student actually liked the teacher and desired a high level of the teacher's attention. The student felt that he was not receiving enough recognition from the teacher and wanted to be appreciated by the teacher. Once the teacher recognized the feelings in John, she was much more successful at understanding his feelings and, in turn, being able to manage his behavior.

TYPES OF DISCIPLINE PROBLEMS

Various types of misbehavior have been categorized by social scientists. Charles (1996) categorized five types of misbehavior: (1) aggression, (2) immorality, (3) defiance of authority, (4) class disruptions, and (5) goofing off (see Figure 1.3). These broad categories of misbehavior represent common areas of inappropriate student behavior typically found in classrooms.

Tomal (1997a) categorized several types of misbehavior based upon a research study with selective teachers in public high schools. Using a questionnaire, teachers were asked to rank-order each of the misbehaviors based on how often they encountered the problem, and also how difficult each disciplinary problem was to manage (see Table 1.1).

While the sample of teachers represented a diverse ethnic background, the majority of teachers taught in schools with a high level of minority students who came from lower socioeconomic status families. These teachers also indicated that they experienced a high incidence of disciplinary problems at the school and desired improved skills in disciplinary management.

The term "disciplinary problem" was defined loosely as any offense or behavior by a student that was deemed, by the teacher, to hinder student learning or to compromise the educational process. Therefore, while

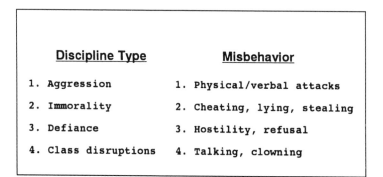

Discipline Type   **Misbehavior**

1. Aggression   1. Physical/verbal attacks

2. Immorality   2. Cheating, lying, stealing

3. Defiance   3. Hostility, refusal

4. Class disruptions   4. Talking, clowning

Figure 1.3. Types of discipline problems.

TABLE 1.1. Rank Order of Discipline Problems.

Discipline Problem	Frequency Rank	Difficulty Rank
Use of profanity	5	7
Defiance or disrespect	3	3
Talking without permission	1	2
Cheating or lying	6	6
Sleeping in class	7	10
Apathy or low motivation	2	1
Harassing other students	7	4
Tardiness or absenteeism	4	4
Verbal fighting	9	8
Physical fighting	10	9

$r = .86.$

most of the descriptions of the disciplinary problems were the typical offenses committed by students in schools today, some of the disciplinary behaviors related to such situations as missed work assignments, apathy, low motivation, careless work, poor attendance, and disinterest in grades.

There was a very high correlation between the frequency of disciplinary problems and degree of difficulty in managing them ($r = .86$). The data indicated that talking without permission was a disciplinary problem that was not only most frequent, but also the most difficult to manage. Apathy or low motivation was another disciplinary problem that was ranked the second highest in frequency and most difficult to manage. The discipline problem of defiance and disrespect was ranked number three for both frequency and difficulty.

While sleeping (a general term used to described dozing off, daydreaming, and the like) was ranked seventh, the teachers ranked it least difficult in management. The least frequent discipline problem rankings included physical fighting and verbal fighting. The teachers also ranked physical and verbal fighting as not being difficult to manage in respect to the other disciplinary problems.

While there were several limitations to this study (e.g., limited sample population, non-random selection), the survey results allowed teachers in follow-up inservice workshops to examine the various types of problems and improve their skills in managing them. While these discipline problems may vary from teacher to teacher and school to school, the list can be helpful as an instructional tool in helping teachers to understand and develop strategies in managing each of them.

DISCIPLINE MODELS

There have been numerous discipline models proposed by researchers to help teachers understand and manage disciplinary problems. While all these models provide useful information for teachers, no model has been fully embraced as a panacea for managing discipline problems in the classroom. There have been many critics of these various models, who suggest that some models are too harsh and demeaning to students, while others are too impractical or lenient. However, these models can be helpful by providing a teacher with strategies and techniques in managing discipline.

Behavioral Modification

The most noted researcher in Behavioral Modification is B. F. Skinner (1902–1990) who conducted numerous experimental studies while at Harvard University. Much of Skinner's work in the 1930s dealt with laboratory experiments in learning using rats and pigeons. He later articulated the results from his experiments and applied them to people.

While Skinner never proposed an actual model for student discipline, his principles and theories have been used by teachers in managing discipline and have been applied by many psychologists and educators in educational institutions. Skinner's behavioral modification is basically a system of techniques of reinforcement and punishment in attempting to shape ideal behavior in students. Skinner largely proposed the use of reinforcing stimulus, punishment, and negative reinforcers to shape behavior.

The positive reinforcers proposed by Skinner consisted of a variety of intrinsic and extrinsic rewards given to students by the teacher. The idea of giving positive reinforcement encourages students to perform desirable behaviors, while the use of punishment attempts to eliminate undesirable behaviors. Positive reinforcers include candy, gold stars, certificates, gestures, and compliments. Examples of punishment include a repetitious writing exercises, standing out in the hall, or suspension. While not utilized in most schools today, corporal punishment is also an example of punishment.

The use of punishment has been sharply criticized by many researchers because they feel punishment produces side effects of fear, hatred, and vengeance in a student. However, some researchers, such as James

Dobson, a licensed psychologist and author, have suggested that corporal punishment is beneficial to administer to children for serious acts (e.g., life-threatening and chronic insubordinate actions). Dobson, in his book, *Dare to Discipline* (1970) and *The New Dare to Discipline* (1992), emphasizes the importance of maintaining a healthy home environment built upon love and control. Dobson suggests that for children ólder than the first grade, other forms of punishment, such as financial deprivation and loss of privileges, be substituted for spanking. While Dobson feels that well-thought out and properly administered spanking can be effective in modifying behavior, he also feels that administering this punishment can be dangerous if not done out of love for the child.

Skinner also proposed the concept of negative reinforcement as an effective means for shaping behavior. The technique of negative reinforcement is an attempt to eliminate an undesirable behavior by eliminating or removing an unfavorable consequence. Negative reinforcement is not the same as punishment, which adds something unfavorable. An example of negative reinforcement might be when a teacher tells the students if they receive the letter grade A on the next test, they will not have to complete the remaining homework assignments. The idea of this type of reinforcement is to encourage the students to perform in a desirable manner by eliminating an unfavorable consequence.

While behavioral modification techniques have been effectively used in altering student behavior, this model has had considerable criticism. Given that behavior modification focuses on observable student behavior, it may be ineffective in dealing with emotional and psychological aspects. If a student has a great deal of anxiety as a result of a dysfunctional home environment, it could be viewed as unethical to temporarily control the student's behavior in the classroom through behavioral modification techniques and avoid addressing the student's inner problem. Moreover, the use of behavioral modification could actually harm students, especially if it is not administered appropriately.

Cooperative Discipline

Much of the knowledge that has evolved from the Cooperative Discipline Model has been an outgrowth of the research of Alfred Adler, Rudolf Dreikurs, Linda Albert, and Jane Nelsen. Most of the educators have utilized Adler's principles to manage student discipline in the classroom. The philosophy of cooperative discipline is based upon the following behavioral concepts: (1) Students are responsible for their behavior; (2) students' behavior is based upon fulfillment of their need of social belonging; and (3) students often misbehave in order to obtain attention, power, or revenge.

Cooperative discipline theory is based upon the notion of democratic teaching, establishing a genuine environment with a sense of belonging for students, and the elimination of students using attention, power, revenge, or apathy as a substitute for their sense of belonging in the classroom. Cooperative discipline attempts to create an environment where students feel stimulated, creative, involved with their peers, and genuinely connected with the class. The use of cooperative discipline involves the attempt to establish positive control through student self-discipline rather than the use of punishment.

While cooperative discipline has many benefits, it has also been viewed as having several limitations. Not all students may want to be a part of a group, some students may resent other misbehaving students receiving special attention, the social goals of students may vary, and determining a student's social needs and desires may be difficult for a teacher.

Reality Therapy

Reality Therapy was first proposed in 1965 by William Glasser, a noted psychiatrist and educator. Glasser wrote about the principles of reality therapy in several books: *Reality Therapy* (1965), *Schools Without Failure* (1969), *The Quality School* (1990), and *The Quality School Teacher* (1993). Glasser's theory is largely based upon a sociological needs theory approach. He emphasizes that students must be responsible for their behavior and that they have choices. He suggests that teachers and students need to conduct group meetings during classroom time to establish rules and procedures and that the teacher should be the leader in maintaining order within the classroom.

Glasser emphasizes the importance of the sociological needs of belonging, love, control, and freedom. Essentially, Glasser reports that if student needs can be met within the classroom, discipline problems will be controlled. Glasser feels that basic student needs include survival, belonging, power, fun, and freedom. His approach is a practical, genuine, and down-to-earth set of principles and guidelines for teachers. Glasser's principles involve the use of collaboration, cooperation, meeting student needs, pursuit of quality, continuous improvement, and a low emphasis on grading and critical evaluation. Providing meaningful and relevant activities for students is a prime aspect of this model.

Many of Glasser's advancements to the Reality Theory appear to be an outgrowth of the Total Quality Management (TQM) movement. TQM can be described as a total dedication to providing quality service for the customer. It was first coined by the Department of Defense and is based upon the principles of Joseph Juran, Philip Crosby, and Edwards Deming.

A criticism of Glasser's model is that teachers do not always have total authority to determine the curriculum and activities for their classes. There are many state and district policies on the selection of subjects, curriculum, and instruction. Many students may dislike certain required subjects. Also, many teachers may not want to allocate precious classroom instructional time for open collaborative-based meetings with students.

The Kounin Model

Jacob Kounin, a psychology professor at Wayne State University, has conducted many research studies on teachers in the classroom. His published work, *Discipline and Group Management in Classrooms* (1977), outlined his principles for managing student discipline. The Kounin Model is based upon the premise that teachers need to become effective in "with-it-ness," overlapping, movement management, and group processing. Kounin defines "with-it-ness" as a teacher's ability to know what is occurring in the classroom at any given moment ("with it") and being alert to the behavior of all the students at any given time. He suggests that skilled teachers are those who are able to promptly deal with misbehavior and anticipate the needs of students.

The term "overlapping" refers to a teacher's ability to handle two or more simultaneous activities within the classroom, an important skill in maintaining discipline. Kounin also feels that teachers need to maintain good balance and activity momentum in the classroom and avoid jerkiness in the flow of student activities. He feels that any time there is a disruption in the flow of activities, confusion and misbehavior can result. He also feels that any delays or fragmentation (slowdown) can hinder the learning environment.

The Kounin Model emphasizes the importance of group dynamics. He suggests that groups be held accountable for their performance, that students be attentive in their learning activities, and that groups maintain focus on an activity. While the Kounin model has been widely received for preventing disciplinary problems, it has been criticized for not being as effective in allowing teachers to expeditiously correct misbehavior

(Charles, 1996). Also, this model may not place enough emphasis on the role of a teacher's personality traits and skills in managing disciplinary problems.

The Positive Discipline Model

Fredric Jones, a psychologist, articulated a Positive Discipline Model in his book *Positive Classroom Discipline* (1987). His model emphasizes the importance of eliminating the minor transgressions such as unauthorized talking and moving around in the classroom. He suggested that these types of misbehaviors constitute the majority of time in managing discipline. His model is built upon the effective use of non-verbal communication, utilizing effective incentive systems, and personalizing cooperation in the classroom.

Jones recommended the use of a three-step approach of praise, promptness, and leave. In this process, teachers praise students for good performance, tell them what to do next, and leave the student to complete the learning activity. He suggested the use of body language techniques to maintain control of students.

A unique aspect of the Positive Discipline Model is the use of an incentive system called Preferred Activity Time (PAT). The PAT system incorporates the use of a point system in which students earn points for good behavior and lose points for inappropriate behavior. While the Positive Discipline Model has similar characteristics to the Kounin Model, Jones focused more on classroom management and the interpersonal relations among the teacher and students. The Positive Discipline Model was especially useful for providing techniques for teachers for eliminating the petty misbehaviors versus dealing with more serious actions such as fighting, foul language, harassment, or horseplay.

Some limitations of the Positive Discipline Model include the failure to acknowledge the roles of teacher-student verbal communication, parental involvement, and incentive systems for motivating good student behavior.

Assertive Discipline

A popular discipline model proposed by Lee Canter (1976) is called Assertive Discipline. This model, which appears to have been built upon earlier theories of discipline, is an attempt to provide teachers with effective student discipline through firmness and a positive approach. Some principles of Assertive Discipline include the importance of setting class-room rules, providing positive recognition to students, and administering consequences when rules are not followed.

The Assertive Discipline Model includes a progressive discipline approach. The student receives progressively harsher actions for offenses. The model also suggests conducting problem-solving conferences between the teacher and the student to agree upon contracts for appropriate behavior. The Model is also effective by allowing teachers to handle problems quickly and consistently through a single system of procedures, rewards, and punishments.

While the Assertive Discipline Model has been a popular model, it has also received criticism for its rigidity for not taking into account extenuating circumstances (Charles, 1996). Also, unlike Glasser's and Dreikur's models, the Assertive Discipline Model has been viewed as undemocratic and authoritarian with little room for student cooperative involvement.

Discipline With Dignity

A discipline model proposed by Richard Curwin and Allen Mendler (1980) is called Discipline with Dignity. The major principles of this model include managing misbehaviors as a natural part of teaching and by implementing it as a long-term process, maintaining student dignity without hindering motivation, and promoting student responsibility. This model has been especially useful for teachers who are concerned with chronically misbehaved students.

Curwin and Mendler suggest that the chronically misbehaved student (less than five percent of the student population) significantly impacts on the entire student population. Therefore, teachers need to focus on this student to effectively manage the entire class. Discipline with Dignity emphasizes student responsibility rather than obedience, student collaboration, consequences for inappropriate behavior, and the importance of allowing student choices in the classroom. This model can provide meaningful methods in helping the chronically misbehaved student over a long-term process.

While this model may be viewed with some criticism (Charles, 1996) because of the tension of teachers in viewing their role, it does provide helpful strategies and techniques for maintaining day-to-day discipline in a classroom. It also has been viewed as being less effective in expeditiously dealing with a disciplinary problem.

CHAPTER 2

Discipline by Negotiation— Developing "Street Smarts"

HUMAN NEEDS AND STUDENT BEHAVIOR

WHILE THERE ARE many different discipline models, most of them have in common an underlying concern regarding the fundamental human needs of children. Students' attitudes and behaviors can often be traced to these human needs. Developing and understanding human needs can be invaluable in motivating students and managing discipline.

There are several theories of human needs. Abraham Maslow (1943) articulated one of the first theories on human needs by classifying them into five levels. The lower-order needs (i.e., first two levels) consist of basic physiological needs, including safety and security. The higher-order needs (i.e., upper three levels) consist of belonging and social needs, esteem and status needs, and self-actualization and fulfillment. Alderfer (1969) modified Maslow's hierarchy by reducing it to three levels: existence, relatedness, and growth. Figure 2.1 illustrates a comparison of Maslow's and Alderfer's needs models. Alderfer's theory, called the E-R-G Model, proposes that people are first interested in satisfying their existence needs (e.g., a combination of physiological and safety needs). Once these lower-order needs are met, a person then strives to meet the relatedness needs (e.g., a combination of social and self-esteem needs). The highest level need, growth (e.g., a combination of ego and self-actualization), involves the continuous desire for learning and developing one's skills and talents to the fullest.

Both of these theories have helped educators in understanding students' motivations and behaviors in the classroom. For example, the lower-level physiological needs (e.g., food, water, sleep, air, and reasonable temperature), are fundamental requirements of life and are important for survival. These needs are virtually universal among all human beings, but may, however, vary in degree of importance from one person to another. Students require varying degrees of sleep, which directly

19

Maslow's Hierarchy	Alderfer's Model
Self Actualization	Growth
Esteem and Status	
	Relatedness
Social & Belonging	
Safety & Security	
	Existence

Figure 2.1. Maslow's hierarchy of needs theory and Alderfer's E-R-G Model.

impacts on students' behaviors and academic performances in the classroom. Some students may have a greater desire for comfortable room temperature than others for an adequate learning environment. Students who are deprived of these most basic physiological needs may exhibit misbehavior in the classroom.

Students whose most basic needs of food and shelter are not met may be more concerned about meeting those needs than learning. For example, an administrator may need to provide food for students who attend an extended-school day program, given that the students may not be able to learn when they are hungry.

A student who has a void in the level of safety and security may also resort to various types of misbehavior if he/she feels his/her safety or security is being threatened. For example, if a student is in fear of his/her life, he/she may bring a gun with him/her to school in order to protect himself/herself. Violating school policies may not be important to the student who feels a need for personal protection. The threat of gang assault may be an overriding factor in his/her behavior in the school. If the student can be assured that his/her environment is safe at the school, the student may decide that carrying a gun is unnecessary.

One of the more powerful human needs for students is the social need. Peer identification is very important for adolescent students. The need to belong and have fun with one's peer group can be a driving need that determines a student's behavior in a classroom. For example, if a student's social need is unsatisfied, he/she may resort to class disruptions, goofing around, and attention-seeking behaviors in order to fulfill this need. Another student whose social need is unsatisfied may feel so isolated that he/she may literally reject the classroom and resent the teacher and fellow students. A teacher recognizing that a need level, such as a social need, is not being met can better equip the teacher to deal with various types of misbehavior.

Once students feel they are socially connecting with their peer group in the classroom, they may then look to fulfill the need level of self-esteem and ego. Students might attempt to fulfill this need by acquiring power and authority. They may resort to aggressive verbal or physical attacks against other students in order to gain power and influence over them.

The relationship of students' social needs and their classroom behaviors has been recognized by Glasser (1965). Glasser felt that peer recognition is a powerful influence on students in the developmental years. Students have the need to be accepted socially and have a positive self-esteem. For example, once a student's social needs are met, he/she will then seek to meet the higher-level needs of self-esteem and status within the classroom. Students might seek attention or they might misbehave in order to obtain peer recognition. Teachers should foster a classroom environment that supports the fulfillment of student needs at all of these levels. For example, the use of cooperative and collaborative learning may be an approach in which students' social and self-esteem needs can be met.

The highest level of need, self-actualization or relatedness, involves providing classroom experiences that allow students to learn and develop their skills and talents to the fullest. Given that higher-level needs are more vague than the primary needs, the use of intrinsic motivational factors (e.g., meaningful learning activities, student responsibility, and challenging exercises) are probably most effective in motivating students (Kohn, 1993).

The students' desires to fulfill their human needs in the classroom involve a multiplicity of factors such as peer-group identification, sense of duty, peer rivalry, desire to learn, attitude toward the teacher and school, and need for attention and affection. If these needs are not met, disciplinary problems can result. Understanding how to meet student human needs can help students act in an acceptable manner.

MOTIVATION AND STUDENT BEHAVIOR

One of the landmark theories of human motivation that can be applied to student discipline is the Two Factor Theory of Motivation proposed by Fredric Herzberg (1966). While Herzberg primarily worked with

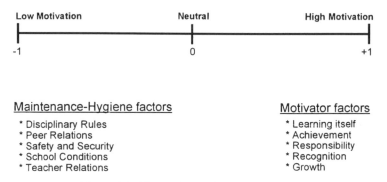

Figure 2.2. *The two factor theory of motivation.*

industrial companies, his theories can also be applied to the educational setting (see Figure 2.2).

Herzberg concluded that people experience good or bad feelings based upon different types of conditions at work. He theorized that different factors will influence motivation based upon workers' views toward these motivational factors.

Herzberg categorized these motivational factors into two groups, maintenance factors and motivational factors. Maintenance factors consisted of relations with supervisors, peer relations, quality of supervision, administrative company policies, work conditions, and reward structures. Motivational factors consisted of the work itself, the possibility of growth and advancement, responsibility, status within the organization, recognition, and achievement.

Herzberg reported that when workers' maintenance factors were not met, they became dissatisfied. These potent dissatisfiers, hygiene factors, must be met at a minimum level of acceptance, or workers will become de-motivated. Once these hygiene factors are in place, workers' motivations will not increase their motivation unless given the higher-level motivational factors.

Herzberg's model can be applied to students in the classroom. If students' maintenance factors, such as school discipline policies, the administration of policies, safety and security, and school conditions, are not met at a reasonable level, students can become dissatisfied and misbehave. The lack of clear-cut school policies and inconsistent, unfair administration of these policies can result in increased disciplinary problems within the entire school.

Like workers in a company, once maintenance factors have been met for students within a school, in order to provide the opportunity for students to become motivated, motivational factors must be provided.

Valence X Expectancy X Instrumentality = Motivation

Figure 2.3. The Expectancy Model.

These motivational factors might include potential for growth and learning, peer recognition, awards and academic achievement, status within the school, and the rewards of future educational opportunities. If motivational factors are not provided, students may never become motivated to grow to higher academic levels.

Another landmark theory, proposed by Victor Vroom (1964), that can be applied to the educational setting is called the Expectancy Model (see Figure 2.3). Vroom theorized that human motivation is based upon the product of three factors: desire for a reward (valence), belief that an effort will result in completion of a task (expectancy), and knowledge that a reward will be obtained upon completion of the task (instrumentality).

When applied to the classroom setting, valence, the first factor, can be viewed as a student's preference for receiving a good grade (e.g., reward). The student may strongly desire a good grade in a class and will be highly motivated to perform. However, if a student lacks this desire and is indifferent because of peer pressure or another external factor, he/she will have a low valence and will not be motivated to achieve, and will consequently be more prone to misbehave.

The second level, expectancy, can refer to a student's belief that his/her effort will result in the achievement of a desired task (e.g., successful completion of tests and homework assignments). For example, if a student feels that spending more time completing homework will result in a better grade on a homework assignment, then the student will spend more time on the homework. However, if the student feels there is not an important relationship between study time and successful completion of homework, he/she will be less motivated.

The third level, instrumentality, relates to a student's belief that a reward can be realistically obtained. For example, the student might believe that a teacher is prejudiced against him/her and no matter how well the student completes his/her homework, the student will never receive an excellent grade. In this case, the student's instrumentality will be low and the result will be low student motivation.

Highly motivated students need to have high levels of all three factors—valence, expectancy, and instrumentality. Vroom theorized that the strength of a person's drive to reach a goal is based upon the

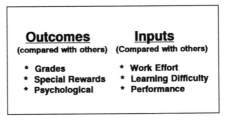

Figure 2.4. The Equity Model.

combination of these three factors, and a supervisor should strive to provide incentives for workers. Likewise, the experiences students obtain in the classroom can directly contribute to their drive for each of these factors. Teachers can help provide these incentives by establishing classroom rules and procedures, fair and consistent evaluations, and reward structures.

A motivational theory which goes beyond just satisfying the needs of people is called the Equity Model (see Figure 2.4). This model (Adams, 1965) suggests there is a direct relationship between how a student behaves and how he/she feels about the teacher's fairness in managing the classroom. Adams theorized that the issue of fairness applies to all types of rewards such as social, economic, and psychological.

The premise of this model is that people will bring inputs into their work (e.g., personal commitment, time, desire, and energy) and expect to receive outcomes (e.g., grades, praise, recognition, and certificates). People will analyze the degree of fairness of receiving their own outcomes as compared to outcomes being received by others. The fairness, or equality, of these factors will be subjectively judged by the person. If the person believes that the outcomes (i.e., rewards) justify his/her degree of input as compared with others then the person will be motivated. However, if the person feels that his/her outcomes are inadequate and unfair, as compared to others, then the person will not be motivated, and disciplinary problems will result.

For example, if a student is contributing a high input of study time but his/her grade is unsatisfactory as compared to his/her peers, an imbalance will result in the student's perception. As a result, the student may contribute less input to learning and more input to harassing his/her classmates and teacher to compensate for his/her feelings of resentment.

If students feel they are overrewarded for their efforts, they may be psychologically more prone to discount and place less value on the reward (i.e., a high grade). For example, if a teacher is too lenient in grading, students may ultimately place less value on learning and may be more prone to misbehave. A good balance of input and output keeps a student motivated and less likely to misbehave.

The social learning theory, developed by Albert Bandura (1977), can be helpful in understanding student motivation and behavior in the classroom. This theory suggests that people obtain information regarding how well they perform by observing their peer group. This concept, called vicarious learning, essentially means "learning through the experiences of others." Bandura suggests that students place greater value on observing the behaviors of teachers than on policies and procedures of the school.

For example, if teachers allow rules to be broken, students will mentally process the actions of the misbehaving students and misbehave themselves. In effect, students are constantly observing their peers within their classroom and the teacher's behavior to ensure that their behavior is consistent with the rules of the classroom. This theory reinforces the importance of reasonable classroom rules and consistency in the administration of these rules.

The notion of motivating students through the establishment of suitable class policies and rules has been reinforced by the work of William Glasser (1990). Glasser emphasized that schools need to pay more attention to providing for the inherent needs of students such as belonging, power, fun, and freedom. He felt that the meeting of these needs was essential to create a healthy classroom learning environment and reduce disciplinary problems.

For example, students need to feel that they are having fun in class, that they have a degree of power, and that they are experiencing meaningful activities that allow them a sense of freedom to explore and learn. Glasser felt that class rules should be consistent with providing an environment that affords the best quality of learning for the students. When rules are broken, the teacher's emphasis should be establishing a quality environment as opposed to power and control. Glasser attempts to resolve disciplinary problems by giving importance to non-punitive interventions and refocusing students' attention on quality of work.

The misbehavior of students may be justified in their minds if specific needs are not met. For example, students may commit acts of immorality such as stealing if their most basic physiological needs of food and shelter are not being met. The student may justify stealing money from another student in order to satisfy this basic physiological need. Likewise, a student who disrupts the class may be trying to satisfy a social need. Understanding the relationship of these various needs theories relative to classroom behavior is a key in managing discipline problems.

NEGOTIATING WITH STUDENTS

Tomal (1997b) conducted a study where he examined the various methods teachers use to manage disciplinary problems. Interview sessions were conducted with teachers about their experiences in handling different types of disciplinary problems. Typical teacher responses to questions about classroom disruption included, "Basically you have to try and get them to do what you want them to do," "Students play games with you and attempt to get something they want—attention, peer recognition, power, less work," and "Students become bored and disinterested with school, which results in inappropriate classroom behaviors to occupy their time." Teachers stated that they experienced significant and overwhelming stress as a result of disciplinary problems and that managing misbehaving students was the most difficult aspect of their work.

This study supported the theories of Curwin and Mendler (i.e., Discipline with Dignity) given that teachers reported that dealing with a few difficult students created significant stress for the teacher and impacted the learning of all the students in the class. Teachers also reported that while a few students caused the majority of disciplinary problems, the teachers needed to manage disciplinary or motivational problems to some degree with all their students.

When teachers were asked questions about student apathy or poor academic performance, typical responses included "Students seem to always want to bargain with you—more time to complete homework, desire another chance to perform work," "They often displace blame to others to avoid responsibility," and "They are always giving you some excuse to give them a break." When asked about a student's response to receiving disciplinary action for an offense, several teachers reported that students would say, "Please give me another chance," or would attempt to receive a reduced or alternate disciplinary action.

Teachers also reported that, except for handling more egregious student offenses, they did not have strong confidence in the effectiveness of the school disciplinarian dean. Many teachers felt that the students eventually came back to their class anyway, or little was actually done to ameliorate the problem. Therefore, most teachers believed that they were ultimately responsible for managing disciplinary problems and that they had to individually manage misbehavior with their own skills and methods.

An analysis of the teachers' responses in this study showed a rather intriguing pattern. The general theme of the disciplinary situations involved a series of interpersonal communications between the teacher and the student with each person taking a positional view. These interactions between the teacher and student had an obvious negotiation element. In a disciplinary situation, teachers would often take a position (i.e., a set of perceptions about desired student behavior), and the student would take a different position. Both parties (i.e., teacher and student) took positions that were generally incongruent with each other. In essence, both parties wanted something and were engaged in a negotiation process to achieve a desired personal outcome. The party that was more skillful in negotiating their position (i.e., street smarts) was generally more successful in achieving their desired outcome.

Teachers were eager to illustrate that not all disciplinary situations were resolved in an expeditious manner. A quick corrective statement by a teacher to a student might temporarily resolve a discipline in the short term but might create long-term problems by the student feeling resentment or hostility. These harbored ill feelings may be manifested in student attitudes of demotivation or apathy. In other cases, a quick corrective statement by a teacher was not always successful in resolving a student problem. For example, when a teacher reprimanded a student for failure to complete an assignment, the student would typically offer a flurry of excuses in an attempt to negotiate a better settlement (i.e., avoidance of personal responsibility and accepting criticism from the teacher).

An analysis of the teachers' responses in this study appear to be similar to adult situations in life such as dealing with a police officer for a traffic violation, going through a tax audit, discussing work performance with a boss, negotiating a business contract, or dealing with a legal dispute. The notion that negotiating is a life process among people and that this process also takes place in the classroom between teachers and students is a reasonable assumption. Every day people engage in interactions with other people and attempt to come to an agreement on something— similar to disciplinary interactions among teachers and students.

Whether or not teachers want to accept the fact that they have to negotiate with their students, they do not really have a choice. As long as people are dealing with people, there will always be an negotiation element.

Regardless of the issues involved, the steps of negotiating in the classroom are similar. This process involves (1) a difference in position on an issue, (2) bargaining of issues, and (3) resolution of the issue. The teacher may desire that a student stop talking to other students and work more diligently on an exercise, while the student may want the freedom to openly talk and avoid the assignment. The student may bargain with the teacher by stating that he/she isn't talking and blame it on someone else in an attempt to win his/her position. The ultimate resolution of the issue will occur based upon who, the teacher or student, is more effective in negotiating.

The idea of Discipline by Negotiation is based upon the premise that students, like all other human beings, embark on a series of interpersonal interactions throughout the day in an effort to meet some underlying need. Negotiation is a life process and all people negotiate every day in their lives.

CHAPTER 3

Student Negotiating Tactics

STUDENT TACTICS AND DISCIPLINE

STUDENTS USE MANY negotiating tactics on a day-to-day basis in the classroom. These negotiating tactics are strategies employed by students in an attempt to bargain for something they want. They negotiate in order to satisfy an inner need such as safety, peer recognition, power, self-esteem, self-actualization, or other sociological desires.

The use of negotiation tactics in the classroom is an outgrowth of learned and conditioned strategies that students have learned from interactions with people in their home and social environment. Students learn that in order to survive in this world they must develop "street smarts" to negotiate with parents, siblings, peers, and the public. Students bring the use of these tactics into the classroom when interacting with their teachers during disciplinary situations.

Student tactics fall into three general categories: offensive, defensive, and avoidance (see Figure 3.1). Offensive tactics are aggressive and attacking-type strategies that students use to bargain a position. Defensive tactics are defending and protecting-type strategies used by students to act in opposition against a teacher's position. Avoidance tactics are denial-type strategies used by students to avoid responsibility for their actions and to avoid receiving a disciplinary penalty. Each category of tactics has distinct characteristics that students use in bargaining with their teachers depending upon the nature of the disciplinary situation.

For example, a student may use offensive tactics when trying to persuade a teacher to allow the student a special privilege or to take advantage of another student to gain power over him/her. Defensive tactics might be used when a student has violated a school rule and attempts to shift the blame to someone else or justify their misbehavior. Students might use avoidance tactics to deny responsibility for an offense and to protect themselves from feeling bad.

29

Offensive Negotiating Tactics

* Emotional Tantrum

* Fait Accompli

* Good Guy, Bad Guy

* Quick Deal

* What If

Defensive Negotiating Tactics

* Forbearance

* Projection

* Rationalization

* One More Chance

Avoidance Negotiating Tactics

* Denial of Reality

* Handicap Syndrome

* Emotional Insulation

* Dumb is Smart, Smart is Dumb

Figure 3.1. *Student negotiating tactics.*

STUDENT OFFENSIVE TACTICS

The offensive tactics used by students include the "emotional tantrum," *"fait accompli,"* "good guy, bad guy," "quick deal," and the "what if." Each of these tactics is used by students to aggressively attempt to negotiate an outcome from a teacher.

Emotional Tantrum

Students use the "emotional tantrum" tactic to draw sympathy and to produce an element of guilt in the teacher. For example, if a student is talking without permission or is suspected of cheating, the student might respond to the teacher with great emotion by yelling, "You're always picking on me!" "You just have it in for me!" or "You just don't like me!" Students use the emotional tantrum tactic to gain attention by using outlandish and emotional behavior, hoping that the teacher will feel sorry for them and make concessions. Concessions might include a sympathetic response, reduced disciplinary action, or preferential treatment.

Students have learned through their early childhood years that the use of emotional tantrums can be a very effective means of getting what they want from their parents. Parents often are inclined to acquiesce to their children's demands in order to stop the child's tantrum or to reduce their own feelings of guilt they might experience as a result of the child's tantrum. A parent may experience personal feelings of guilt because of their desire to discipline their children but not to the extent of driving the child to act out of control. If the parent gives in to the child's demands because of the emotional tantrum, this will have reinforcing consequences and the child will be conditioned to use this tactic in the future.

An example might include a situation when a child is in a store and wants candy from his/her mother and the mother refuses to give the child the candy. The child screams and cries until the mother gives in. The mother's intentions are to pacify the child, avoid a public scene, and eradicate her feelings of guilt and stress by compromising her position. The use of this tactic can easily carry over to the classroom. A young teenage female student may create a scene through her emotional crying to her teacher in an attempt to obtain something she desires. Her teacher may feel sorry for her and feel partially responsible for producing this behavior and may be more inclined to accommodate her.

Human beings often can be very sympathetic to other people who utilize the emotional tantrum tactic. Students have also learned the use of this tactic by observing adult role models. It is not uncommon for parents and other public authorities to participate in an emotional tantrum in order to emphasize a specific position. For example, children may witness an argument between their parents where the father resorts to hostility to enforce his rules in the home. Children learn that this behavior can be effective for adults and in turn mimic the behavior.

Teacher union representatives may utilize this tactic in bargaining for a better contract. Public officials may utilize the emotional tantrum to emphasize a specific position in the media. Movies and television can also dramatize the use of this tactic by showing scenes in which actors depict emotional outbursts to create power positions in order to win a battle against their opponent.

Fait Accompli

The tactic of *"fait accompli"* (or accomplished fact) is used by a student to attempt to bring finality to an issue. For example, the student may make statements such as "This is the best that I can do," "I just don't know anymore," "Sorry, I didn't have enough time to finish the assignment—you'll have to take it the way it is," or "This is my very best effort—I can't do anymore." The student's real motive for making these statements is to obtain a final grade and avoid doing any more work. The teacher may be tempted to accept the student's statement as truthful and accommodate the student's request unless the teacher understands the student's ploy. By using the fait accompli tactic, the student is attempting to manipulate the teacher into giving in to their position.

Like the emotional tantrum tactic, the *fait accompli* tactic is used throughout society. For example, a parent may give their child an ultimatum such as requiring the child to be in bed at a certain time, but the parent doesn't enforce the command. The child soon realizes that the parent is just using the tactic as a ploy to get the child to bed but that the child can always negotiate extra time.

Retail stores—car dealers, furniture outlets, and entertainment product stores—often use the *fait accompli* tactic by posting prices on their products in an attempt to persuade their customers to pay the listed price even though they are willing to negotiate a lesser price. The wise consumer knows that many items are negotiable and doesn't fall for this tactic.

The *fait accompli* tactic can be an effective strategy for a student attempting to bluff a teacher. For example, the student may tell his/her teacher that he/she absolutely refuses to obey a command. The student may be simply testing the teacher to see how much misbehavior he/she can get away with.

Good Guy, Bad Guy

The "good guy, bad guy" tactic needs at least two students to play. For example, an abrasive student might begin talking in an obnoxious manner to the teacher, demanding more time for the class to complete an assignment. The student creates a strong emotional stress reaction in the teacher. After a while, a soft-spoken student follows up the argument by talking in a gentle and relaxed manner, humbly making the same request as the obnoxious student. The teacher may be prone to give in to the second student simply because of the manner in which the student behaves. The idea of this tactic is to arouse the teacher emotionally and create tension so that the teacher can end the unpleasant situation by giving in to the nice student.

This tactic is a very effective tactic when used skillfully. The origination of this tactic might be traced to police work. The "good cop, bad cop" tactic is used in a situation where one police officer is abrasive and intimidating to a suspect; then, after a while, the good cop takes over and offers the suspect a cup of coffee and talks nicely to him/her. The intention of the good cop is to soften up the suspect and befriend him/her in order to get information or an admission of guilt.

The Quick Deal

The "quick deal" is a tactic used by students to avoid disciplinary action or to get something they want by quickly apologizing or attempting to distract the teacher by getting the teacher off the subject. For example, the student might say, "Oh, let me run to my locker," "I just need two minutes to finish this homework," or "I won't misbehave again." The teacher may be caught off-guard because of the pressure of the situation and regretfully accommodate the student's request.

Students may use this particular tactic if they feel the teacher is distracted or preoccupied with other activities. The tactic can be effective in order to obtain additional time to complete work or to avoid a more serious penalty for the misbehavior. For example, if a student commits a disciplinary offense and knows he/she will be punished, he/she may offer his/her own disciplinary penalty in order to avoid a more serious one from the teacher. The student may also state that he/she will never do the act again and plead for mercy and exoneration. Students may intentially use this tactic even if they know they will get caught. They rationalize their behavior by thinking that it is easier to ask for forgiveness than to ask for permission given that the consequences of their actions are less than the reward.

The What If

The "what if" tactic is a negotiating ploy used by students to gain power and win a position. For example, students may bargain for a lesser disciplinary action for violating a school policy by offering an alternative course of action. The student might say "If I behave myself the rest of the week, would you let me off this time?" The student is attempting to persuade the teacher by his/her "what if" suggestions.

Another example is a situation when a student intentionally does not complete an assignment. The student might try to obtain more time to complete it instead of accepting a failing grade, by giving a "What if I were to . . . offer." Knowing that he/she is likely to fail the assignment, the student makes a bid to salvage his/her grade by getting another chance. The "what if" tactic can be very effective in seeking out information from a teacher regarding the completion of assignments.

The "what if" tactic can also be a very effective way of negotiating when students arrive late or enroll late in a particular class. The student may make statements such as, "What if I make up the work," or "What if I complete additional work for extra credit," in an attempt to bargain with the teacher. It is not uncommon for students to use the "what if" tactic in front of the entire class in suggesting to a teacher that an alternative type of test be given instead of a traditional written examination. The "what if" tactic can be very effective in bargaining with a teacher given that this tactic often distracts the teacher from the main issue.

STUDENT DEFENSIVE TACTICS

Student defensive tactics include "forbearance," "projection," "rationalization," and "one more chance." Students use defensive tactics to defend themselves from criticism or potential disciplinary action by creating defense ploys.

Forbearance

The use of "forbearance" is used by students to make time work to their advantage. For example, a student may attempt to gain more time to complete an assignment or to delay disciplinary action. In another example, a teacher might give the class a deadline to complete an assignment. When the deadline arrives, the teacher asks the students to turn in the assignments. If a student hasn't completed the assignment, the student might use the forbearance tactic by stating "Oh, I'm sorry, I put my assignment in my backpack—I'll have to find it and give it to you later." The teacher may grant the student's request and carry on with collecting the rest of the class assignments and forgetting about the student, thereby unintentionally giving him/her more time to finish the assignment. The student is simply buying time, hoping that the teacher will become preoccupied or distracted with other activities.

The use of this tactic can be an effective way of obtaining a student desire in the classroom. For example, the student might use this tactic in an attempt to obtain a lesser disciplinary action for an offense he/she has committed. The student may be absent from school and attempt to use time to his/her advantage by hoping the teacher may forget about the disciplinary incident or decrease the seriousness of the incident. Phrases such as, "Let bygones be bygones" or "Time heals all wounds" are common phrases of this tactic.

The essence of using "forbearance" as a tactic is that "patience is a virtue" and that time can be used to one's advantage. Students have also found that this tactic can be very effective in dealing with their peers. For example, a girl may "play hard to get" or put off her boyfriend in an attempt to make herself more desirable to him. People have learned that if time is plentiful, they can create a competitive edge over the other party. People generally do not want to be pressured into something, and will create the illusion of having plentiful time in negotiating with another party to obtain a better settlement.

Projection

The use of "projection" is a tactic used by students to direct or project his/her feelings or behaviors onto another person. This psychological attempt by a student can be an effective means to distort the facts of an issue. For example, a student might state, "He hit me, I didn't hit him," "She was talking to me—I wasn't talking," or "I'm not being disrespectful—you're being disrespectful." The student attempts to avoid responsibility by displacing the problem onto someone else.

This tactic is commonly used between children at home. Children will often blame each other for their own behavior knowing that it will be one person's word against another. The use of projection has also been a common technique between parents. A father might state to his spouse that they should go home because she is tired. In reality, he is actually tired, but he is projecting his feelings onto her in order to compensate for his failure to admit his own feelings. The father may state this in the presence of children, and children eventually learn that this tactic can be an effective means to cover up one's own feelings or perceived inadequacies.

Rationalization

The "rationalization" tactic is used by a student in an attempt to convince the teacher his/her behavior is "rational" in order to justify an unacceptable behavior. A student may use this defense mechanism as a tactic to distract the teacher from the real issue. For example, a student may attempt to justify his/her inappropriate behavior by stating that other teachers allow the behavior in their classrooms. A typical response may be, "Mrs. Smith doesn't care when I do this—why should you?" or "No other teachers have a problem with me." The use of this tactic shifts the attention off the student and onto the teacher and other teachers.

The One More Chance

The "one more chance" tactic is a popular strategy used by students in the classroom. Students will often attempt to negotiate with teachers by asking for another chance in correcting their own behavior. Typical statements might include, "Oh, please let me do the assignment again, and I'll turn it in tomorrow," or "Please give me a break; I promise I'll never do it again." Students will often plead their case by using the "one more chance" tactic, which can be very effective in persuading teachers.

The student knows that if he/she offers an option for a teacher in a disciplinary case, the teacher may opt to accept the student's offer rather going through all the work of completing disciplinary forms or carrying through with disciplinary action against the student. Students seek to appeal to a teacher's sense of mercy by pleading for another chance.

The "one more chance" tactic is a commonly used tactic in society. Children have observed the use of this tactic in the media by accused criminals pleading for mercy in front of a courtroom judge or their older siblings' pleas to their parents for another chance.

STUDENT AVOIDANCE TACTICS

Student avoidance tactics include "denial of reality," "handicap syndrome," "emotional insulation," and the "dumb is smart; smart is dumb." These tactics can be used by the student to avoid taking responsibility or accepting a penalty for their behavior.

Denial of Reality

The "denial of reality" tactic is often used by a student to protect himself/herself from negative feelings or disciplinary action by refusing to admit to his/her own misbehavior. This tactic can be used by both high-achieving students or students with a low self-esteem. These students use the tactic to protect their egos. High-achieving students may utilize this tactic as a defense mechanism since they do not want to confront the reality of not achieving a desired behavior or standard. Likewise, a student with a low self-esteem may condition himself/herself to deny his/her chronic pattern of misbehavior in order to avoid the associated negative feelings.

Students use this tactic to avoid responsibility. For example, if a student is suspected of stealing, the student may simply deny the theft in an effort to avoid prosecution. The use of this tactic can be an effective strategy given that it often leaves doubt in the teacher's mind unless the teacher has concrete evidence against a student. Without absolute proof, the teacher may be inclined to avoid taking disciplinary action against a student.

Handicap Syndrome

Students use the "handicap syndrome" tactic as a method of legitimizing their misbehavior and avoiding responsibility and disciplinary action. A student might respond to a teacher through a victim-mentality position by identifying a real or imagined handicap as an excuse to compensate for not performing to a desired expectation. For example, a student might make reference to a legitimate physical or learning disability as an excuse for their lack of academic performance or appropriate behavior. Other excuses might include a dysfunctional home environment, lack of aptitude, or overinvolvement in an outside activity (e.g., part-time jobs, sports). Typical student excuses for poor behavior/performance include, "I can't do this homework—I've got to work every night," "I'm late for school because I wasn't feeling well," or "Come on, give me a break. You know I am dyslexic!"

The handicap syndrome tactic may be used in conjunction with an attempt to obtain more time to complete a homework assignment or to perform less quality work. Students who resort to using this tactic may have learned its effectiveness from their experiences at home. For example, a child who has a father with a bad back may see the father use this condition as his excuse for not going to work. While the father's back is a legitimate problem, he is embellishing the condition in order to avoid being responsible and as an excuse for his laziness.

A student might use this same tactic to compensate for his/her fear of failure of an assignment. To prevent embarrassment in front of his/her classmates, if the student does not complete the assignment, he/she may blame it on his/her disability. Students understand that this tactic can be effective because it creates doubt in the teacher's mind as to the legitimacy of the student's excuse.

Emotional Insulation

The "emotional insulation" tactic is used by students to withdraw into passivity to protect themselves from inner painful feelings and avoid disciplinary action. In essence, the student "shuts down" and refuses to deal with the reality of the situation. This tactic can be effective as an extreme technique of behavior, given that the tactic portrays a student who is entirely insubordinate and has total disregard for any consequences.

For example, a student might use this tactic to send a signal to the teacher that he/she is willing to go to any extreme, such as receiving a failing grade or being kicked out of the class, in an effort to gain concessions from the teacher. The student may also use this tactic to create feelings of compassion in the teacher. The teacher may feel sorry for the student and shift his/her focus to comforting the student rather than focusing on the misbehavior. The student, by using this tactic, is able to effectively defer the teacher's attention from the disciplinary issue to the student's emotional condition.

The Dumb Is Smart; Smart Is Dumb

Students might use "the dumb is smart; smart is dumb" tactic by acting innocent, naive, or ignorant about the rules and policies of the school in an attempt to avoid a penalty for their misbehavior. For example, the student might violate a school policy and then plea bargain with the teacher by indicating that he/she didn't know about the school policy or that the teacher never informed him/her about the policy. If a student fails to do an assignment, he/she may state that he/she didn't hear the teacher give the assignment, or he/she didn't understand it.

The tactic is used to distract the teacher from the real issue and avoid responsibility. Students have observed this tactic in the media. For example, years ago a popular television show entitled *Columbo* featured the main character as a bumbling investigator who was able to obtain a great deal of information by pretending to be dumb and ignorant. Columbo was able to obtain information because he was able to persuade people to assume a helping role and freely give information.

Students who have exceptional acting abilities can utilize this tactic very effectively in pleading their case to a teacher. For example, a student may be in the classroom and lack the motivation to complete an assignment. The student may use the "dumb is smart; smart is dumb" tactic by stating to the teacher he/she doesn't understand the problem, with the hope that the teacher will do the problem for him/her. Another example is when a student may be guilty of violating a school policy such as wearing inappropriate dress or bringing inappropriate paraphernalia into the school building and then pleads innocence saying that he/she never knew of the policy.

CHAPTER 4

Teacher Negotiating Countertactics

USING TEACHER COUNTERTACTICS

WHEN TEACHERS ARE confronted with tactics by their students, they are forced to rely upon their own arsenal of countertactics. Countertactics are the teacher's weapons of defense to bargain with students in reaching a settlement on a disciplinary issue. In essence, the student is attempting to get something he/she wants, and the teacher, in turn, attempts to obtain his/her own desires.

While teachers tend to naturally develop countertactics when faced with various tactics by students, having an understanding of the countertactics available and developing skills in using them can be very effective in managing discipline problems and motivating students. The key is to be able to recognize the tactic being used by the student, select the most effective countertactic, and then reach a collaborative settlement with the student.

Three categories of countertactics coincide with the student offensive, defensive, and avoidance tactics. These countertactics incorporate various strategies and tactics in bargaining with students as illustrated in Figure 4.1.

TEACHER OFFENSIVE COUNTERTACTICS

Teacher offensive countertactics are used in response to the "emotional tantrum," "*fait accompli*," "good guy, bad guy," "quick deal," and the "what if" student tactics. These countertactics can be used to bargain with students who use aggressive tactics.

Emotional Tantrum Countertactic

When teachers are confronted with the tactic of the emotional tantrum,

41

Student Offensive Tactics	Teacher Countertactics
* Emotional Tantrum	* Ignore tactic, confront emotionalism, focus on facts
* Fait Accompli	* Escalate expectation, use what if tactic
* Good Guy, Bad Guy	* Use fait accompli tactic, change to different subject
* Quick Deal	* Avoidance, Forbearance, or confront the tactic
* What If	* Use what if tactic, ignore it, or fait accompli

Student Defensive Tactics	Teacher Countertactics
* Forbearance	* Use conditional response, or what if tactic
* Projection	* Refer to counselor, or third party mediation
* Rationalization	* Use fait accompli, Positive reinforcement, or counseling
* One More Chance	* Use Forbearance, ignore tactic, or confront the behavior/tactic

Student Avoidance Tactics	Teacher Countertactics
* Denial of Reality	* Refer to counseling, use forbearance tactic
* Handicap Syndrome	* Ignore tactic, use positive reinforcement, or what if
* Emotional Insulation	* Positive reinforcement, use what if tactic, parent conference, or counseling
* Dumb is Smart, Smart is Dumb	* Confront behavior/tactic, avoid giving into the tactic counseling

Figure 4.1. Teacher negotiating countertactics.

a number of different emotional reactions can be felt by the teacher. The teacher may feel guilt, sympathy, emotional rage, or resentment toward the student. The emotional tantrum act in itself can create a very unpleasant situation if done in a classroom setting. Not only does the behavior impact upon the student and teacher, but the entire class is affected by the time wasted during the disciplinary incident.

The teacher can utilize a number of countertactics when confronted with the "emotional tantrum," such as ignoring the tantrum, sticking to the facts of the situation, not allowing the behavior to produce an emotional reaction in the teacher, or by confronting the validity of the statement. The teacher might also confront the unacceptable behavior and privately address the misbehavior with the student.

For example, if the student displays an emotional tantrum, the teacher could simply counter with the tactic of "forbearance." Forbearance can be used to give the teacher time to deal with the student's behavior by simply asking the student to stay calm with the promise of privately discussing the matter at a later time. The use of forbearance allows the teacher to defer confronting the disciplinary matter to a later time so the incident doesn't escalate into a more serious situation.

When dealing with the emotional tantrum, it is important for the teacher to focus on the facts of the situation and not become sidetracked by participating in an emotional exchange with the student. The beginning teacher might be tempted to engage in an emotional discussion with a student, which could get out of control. The beginning teacher may also experience an overwhelming sense of guilt by feeling that he/she might have contributed to the student's behavior.

Many teachers, given that they have great concern for their students as human beings, may opt to feel some sense of responsibility for students' behaviors and may want to apologize and try to accommodate the students' needs. A common reaction may be for the teacher to embark in concession making by giving in to some of the demands of the student in an effort to compromise for the teacher's own personal feelings of guilt. Teachers need to be careful not to fall into the trap of letting the student's tactic produce the natural human feelings of wanting to nurture the student.

A student might use the emotional tantrum, for example, in an attempt to obtain an extra day to turn in an assignment. The quick and easy response by the teacher might be to accommodate the student. However, this temptation should be avoided; otherwise, the use of this tactic will be reinforced by the teacher, and students will continue to use this tactic to take advantage of the teacher.

Fait Accompli Countertactic

When a student uses the "*fait accompli*" tactic, he/she is attempting to bring finality to an issue. For example, a student may make the statement, "This is the best I can do," in an attempt to justify his/her poor behavior or performance. While the teacher may be tempted to use the "emotional tantrum" in reaction to the student's excuses, it is more appropriate to ignore the tactic and maintain an adult position.

Another countertactic a teacher can effectively utilize when faced with this tactic is the "what if" tactic. If the student states that this is the best that he/she can do, the teacher may respond by stating, "What if I were to give you an extra day to complete the assignment more thoroughly?" By responding with this countertactic, the teacher allows the student to continue to complete the assignment and improve upon his/her performance. While the teacher may in fact be accommodating the student, the teacher will be able to allow the student to save face and improve his/her learning. In essence, the teacher gives the student another chance by offering a choice with the hope that the student will continue learning rather than giving up. The teacher can confront the student using the *"fait accompli"* tactic by indicating he/she understands the tactic being used and that it is being used as an excuse for justifying the student's inappropriate behavior. The teacher may also confront the student and request that the tactic not be used anymore as a ploy and encourage the student to be upfront with his/her intentions.

The Good Guy, Bad Guy Countertactic

The "good guy, bad guy" tactic takes at least two students to play. For example, if an entire class is confronting a teacher for reduced homework, a boisterous, disruptive student might make demands and purposely create emotional tension in the teacher. After a while, a soft-spoken student may intervene on behalf of the disruptive student and bargain for the same reduced homework, hoping the teacher will soften and concede.

In this situation, the teacher has many countertactics available. The teacher may counter this tactic by recognizing what is happening, resisting the tendency to give in, or resorting the tactic of *fait accompli*. The use of *fait accompli* can bring quick closure to the situation by stating to the students that the issue is non-negotiable. The teacher at this point can move on to another topic.

It is important that teachers use the appropriate countertactic for a given student tactic. For example, if a teacher were to use a "what if" tactic to counter a "good guy, bad guy" tactic, the entire negotiation session might escalate out of control. The "what if" tactic could not only incite a long discussion on various options, but allow the students to obtain control over the situation.

It is not prudent to always use the same countertactic for a "good buy, bad guy" tactic. For example, if the teacher used the *"fait accompli"* tactic every time, the teacher may be adopting a dictatorial setting in the class that could stifle the free expression and learning of the students. Using different countertactics can be productive in maintaining balance and a collaborative classroom environment.

Quick Deal Countertactic

When a teacher is faced with the "quick deal" tactic, it is important that the teacher quickly recognize that negotiating in this situation can often produce extreme outcomes. For example, if a student states that he/she wants to quickly run to his/her locker and the teacher concedes, he/she may be viewed as giving preferential treatment or being inconsistent in classroom management. The teacher needs to be careful about creating negative impressions for the entire class. Also, although allowing a student to run to his/her locker may appear as an innocent request, the student may have other intentions in mind such as meeting another student or committing some mischievous act.

When faced with the "quick deal," the teacher has to make a judgement call. The teacher should resist the tendency to give in to the quick deal and make use of the forbearance tactic. For example, the teacher might ask the student to go to his/her locker after class. The teacher might confront the tactic by talking with the student or requesting that the student become more organized. Often, if the teacher further explores the student's motives behind the use of the quick deal, the teacher may soon discover insightful information.

What If Countertactic

The "what if" tactic is a common strategy used by students but can be easily countered by the teacher. For example, if the student intentionally does not complete an assignment, the student might try to obtain more time to complete it instead of accepting a failing grade. The teacher might counter this tactic by ignoring the statement, suggesting a teacher–parent conference, or by requesting that the student do additional work. In essence, the teacher counters the "what if" tactic with his/her own what if tactic.

Other options in countering the "what if" tactic include the teacher stating, "What if next time you complete your assignment on time and receive a better grade?" The "what if" tactic as used by the student can be very annoying to the teacher, and the teacher must be careful not to become distracted or irritated with the student, which could serve to escalate the problem.

TEACHER DEFENSIVE COUNTERTACTICS

The teacher defensive countertactics are used in response to the "forbearance," "projection," "rationalization," and "one more chance" student tactics. Defensive tactics contain an element of student manipulation in denying responsibility for their behavior.

Forbearance Countertactic

Given that the basic premise of the forbearance tactic is to allow the student to obtain more time, recognizing the use of this tactic is foremost in countering it. If a teacher is able to quickly recognize the use of this tactic, he/she will not be caught off guard, and he/she will be more effective in negotiating with the student.

When a student uses this tactic, it may be difficult for the teacher to discern whether the student is sincere or whether the student is using this excuse as a genuine tactic. For example, if a student does not have his/her homework when asked by the teacher and the student responds, "It's somewhere in my backpack—give me a few moments and I can find it," the student may be simply buying time, hoping the teacher might be distracted and then forget about the request. The use of this tactic can be effective when classroom activities are very busy and the teacher can be easily distracted by other activities within the room. A countertactic by the teacher might include a condition on the request such as, "If you don't find the homework, make sure you stay after class and talk to me." This might be an effective approach in determining whether the student's excuse is real. The student might opt to quickly respond, "No, that's OK, let's forget it," as opposed to the obvious, needing to stay after class. In essence, the teacher has countered with the *"fait accompli"* tactic, which brings the situation to closure.

Another example where the "forbearance" tactic is used by students is when a student bargains for more time when taking a test. Students will often use this tactic in an attempt to postpone the test. The best response by the teacher may simply be to recognize that the tactic is being used and not give in.

Projection Countertactic

The "projection" tactic, when utilized by a student, can be one of the more difficult tactics for a teacher to counter. Given that this tactic has a psychological underpinning, the student attempts to relate or "project" his/her feelings to another person to compensate for the student's own dysfunction.

For example, if a student pushes another student, he/she might respond by stating, "I didn't push the student; the student pushed me." Obviously, this can be a difficult situation for the teacher if there are no witnesses involved. At this point, the teacher may have to rely upon the statements of the two students involved if there are no witnesses. A countertactic for this situation might include a counseling session. In the counseling session, the teacher, working with a disciplinary administrator, might be able to sort through the situation and obtain the actual facts. A student who utilizes the projection tactic may routinely use it as a form of denial. In situations where the use of this tactic is more clear, and the teacher recognizes it, then the teacher might use a countertactic such as third-party intervention (i.e., school psychologist).

For example, if a student is yelling in the classroom and the teacher asks the student to please stop, the student might respond, "I am not yelling, you are yelling." This tactic is a defense mechanism created by the student to shift the focus off his/her behavior. Psychological intervention can be useful in exploring the underlying reasons for the use of this tactic as well as helping the student to recognize and take responsibility for his/her own behavior.

The teacher may also counsel with the student after class. Confronting a student in front of the class may only escalate the problem, and the teacher needs to be careful to protect the student's psyche. The teacher can use the "forbearance" tactic and tell the student that the problem will be discussed later. This will allow time for the student to become more calm and have a chance to think over the situation.

Rationalization Countertactic

The "rationalization" tactic is a common tactic used by students attempting to defend their behavior. A teacher may counter this tactic by using *"fait accompli."* For example, the teacher might state that the student's rationalizing is unacceptable and that the student must take responsibility for his/her own behavior. The use of *"fait accompli"* takes a "zero tolerance" approach in dealing with the tactic. If the student breaks a school rule, for example, the student must take the consequences.

A teacher can also use the "what if" tactic to counter the rationalization tactic. The teacher might respond to a student who is rationalizing his/her behavior by stating, "What if I were to talk to the other teachers regarding this matter?" or "What if I were to give everyone a break?"

The One More Chance Countertactic

The "one more chance" is a tactic that is commonly used by students in order to attempt to negotiate another opportunity to correct their behavior. Common expressions include, "Oh, please give me a break," or "I promise I'll never do it again." However, even though this basic tactic is obvious, teachers may have a tendency to give in to their demands. Teachers can utilize a number of countertactics such as being obstinate, ignoring the student, terminating the discussion, or confronting the student. The teacher may respond to the student by indicating if he/she were to give the student another chance, then he/she would have to give all students another chance and consistency is important. In essence, the teacher is countering the tactic by being obstinate and not giving in to the student's demands.

The "one more chance" tactic can be difficult to counter since the teacher's natural inclination is to help students, and when the student is personalizing their request and pleading for mercy, it is a big temptation for a teacher to give in. Giving in to this tactic can have reinforcing consequences. Once a teacher starts giving in to this obvious tactic, the student may continue to use this tactic as an excuse for his/her unacceptable behavior or academic performance. The teacher must be able to separate the true issues of the student's request versus the tactic that is being utilized.

At times, it may be necessary for a teacher to negotiate with the student and develop a compromise, but the teacher should resist the student's use of a tactic as a means of concession making. In other words, the teacher, when negotiating with a student, must deal with the issue (i.e., misbehavior) with the student and avoid the tactic that is being utilized. The teacher may confront the student by requesting that the discussion stay focused on the issues as opposed to the tactic being used. The tactic may be a mere distraction to avoid discussing the real underlying causes for the unacceptable behavior.

TEACHER AVOIDANCE COUNTERTACTICS

Denial of Reality Countertactic

Students use the "denial of reality" tactic to avoid taking responsibility for their own behavior or to avoid disciplinary action. The teacher can use the "forbearance" countertactic, since the teacher may want to wait and deal with the situation later if the denial is being made in front of the student's peers. Talking with the student privately may resolve the matter more appropriately without embarrassment to the student. Confronting a student in front of the class could only intensify the problem and create resentment in the student toward the teacher. Sending the student to the school psychologist or counselor may be another alternative for the teacher if the student uses this tactic on a chronic basis.

Handicap Syndrome Countertactic

The "handicap syndrome" tactic is a common strategy used by students to justify their unacceptable behavior or poor performance. When encountering this tactic, the teacher needs to carefully analyze the situation and determine whether the student's excuse is justified. If the teacher concludes that there is no real justification for the excuse, then the teacher can respond with a number of countertactics.

For example, if the student is stating that he/she cannot complete an assignment more thoroughly because of his/her lack of ability, the teacher can counter this tactic by taking an obstinate position and not agreeing with the student. The teacher might also ignore the student's excuse and continue talking as if he/she did not hear it.

The teacher can counter the "handicap syndrome" tactic by using the "what if" tactic. The "what if" tactic can be a very effective means of bargaining by offering the student other options in getting the work done. For example, the teacher may offer a choice to the student of working with other students cooperatively, spending more time with the teacher, or using supplemental resources.

Students who have legitimate disabilities may be more prone to utilize this tactic as an excuse for their unacceptable behavior. It is not uncommon for a student with a legitimate problem to use the problem as an excuse for his/her lack of motivation or indifference in performing school work or good behavior. While the teacher needs to recognize a student's legitimate problem, the teacher must not fall victim to the student's use of the legitimate problem as a negotiating ploy. The teacher might also try the use of praise and reinforcement by recognizing the positive behaviors of the student. Determining this situation may be difficult to sort out for the teacher and requires a careful balance with each unique incident.

Giving in to a student's demand can have reinforcing consequences. The student may use this excuse every time he/she has difficulty with a problem or to compensate for his/her behavior. Use of this type of tactic reinforces a victim mentality in the student. The teacher needs to avoid reinforcing this victim mentality and should ignore the behavior. The teacher should also be careful not to confront the legitimate concern and belittle the student.

Emotional Insulation Countertactic

The "emotional insulation" tactic can be difficult for a teacher to counter. When a student "shuts down" and becomes obstinate, the teacher can easily become frustrated while trying to open up discussion. The teacher can counter this tactic with the use of the "what if" tactic. The teacher might respond with a comment such as, "What if I were to spend extra time with you and the situation?" In this way the teacher might begin to reestablish communication. The teacher may be forced to salvage the situation by allowing the student to save face, rather than allow the student to shut down.

The teacher may need to focus on the student's self-esteem and provide extra attention and reinforcement as a way for the student to deal with his/her emotional insulation. The teacher should try using praise and reinforcement in recognizing the student's positive qualities as a way to re-establish rapport with the student.

Using this tactic may also indicate deep-rooted psychological problems in the student, and the teacher may want to refer the student to the school psychologist. A student who "shuts down" with a teacher may also have outside personal problems that the teacher may need to discuss with the student.

Dumb Is Smart; Smart Is Dumb

The "dumb is smart; smart is dumb" tactic is often used by students to justify their misbehavior with an excuse so that they can avoid taking responsibility for their behavior. Students may say that they did not understand a school policy or hear an assignment, but this tactic is used to distract the teacher from the real issue (i.e., misbehavior) and avoid responsibility. The teacher might counter this tactic by ignoring it. The teacher could validate his/her position by giving proof that the student knew of a policy or assignment.

If, for example, the teacher uses this tactic in an attempt to get the student to complete his/her assignment, the teacher should not fall into this trap and recognize the tactic that is being used to manipulate the teacher. The teacher should be careful not to confront the tactic and get pulled into an never-ending discussion with the student. The teacher needs to recognize the tactic and counter it quickly by sticking to the facts of the incident.

The use of countertactics by teachers is inevitable. Recognizing a given tactic when presented by a student can be useful for a teacher in selecting the most appropriate countertactic to resolve the matter. Experienced teachers may learn the use of countertactics naturally over a period of time. However, learning to better recognize the various student tactics and developing skills in negotiations can assist the teacher in managing classroom discipline problems.

TEACHER DISCIPLINE STYLES

When teachers manage disciplinary problems in the classroom they develop a discipline style. Much like the administrator who develops a defined leadership and conflict management style (Blake & Mouton, 1969; Kilmann & Thomas, 1977), teachers handle student disciplinary problems with different styles (Tomal, 1997b). The discipline styles are based upon the degree of the teacher's *enforcing* of rules and *supporting* of students (see Figure 4.2).

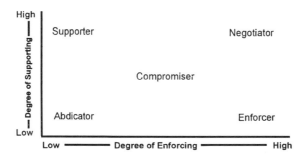

Figure 4.2. *Teacher disciplinary styles.*

The enforcing term is defined as the degree of assertiveness a teacher uses in disciplining students. A teacher who has enforcing attributes places great value on asserting his/her position. Likewise, a teacher who has little concern for enforcing places little emphasis on asserting his/her own position.

The supporting term is defined as the degree to which a teacher accommodates the student. A teacher who has supporting attributes places great value on accommodating the student. The teacher with unsupporting attributes places little value on accommodating the student.

Based upon the combination of the enforcing and supporting attributes, a teacher's style can be categorized into five primary styles—the enforcer, supporter, abdicator, compromiser, and negotiator. Characteristics of these discipline styles are listed in Figure 4.3.

Enforcer

If a teacher has a high degree of enforcing and low degree of supporting, the teacher's style can be called the "enforcer." This teacher is much like a dictator in demanding that his/her students obey his/her rules and

Supporter

* Seeks harmony
* Helpful, gracious
* Indecisive
* Evasive
* Personal
* Unassertive

Negotiator

* Seeks resolution
* Win-win approach
* Objective
* Responsible
* Committed
* Collaborates

Compromiser

* Manipulative
* Inconsistent
* Wishy-washy
* Limits creativity
* Gives and takes
* Open-ended

Abdicator

* Does nothing
* Avoids problems
* Reclusive
* Ignores students
* Bottled-up
* Apathetic

Enforcer

* Self-righteous
* Intimidating
* Controlling
* Threatening
* Demeaning
* Dictatorial

Figure 4.3. Characteristics of teacher disciplinary styles.

allows little room for discussions. The enforcer's attitude is "It is my way or the highway!" This style is very directive and assertive.

The enforcer takes a zero tolerance approach to disciplinary problems. The enforcer style is characteristic of teachers who take a hard-line approach with their students and give them little leeway. They make comments like "The students know the rules in the class and if they break them they know the consequences," and "I run a tight ship in my classroom—there's little room for approaching a disciplinary problem on an individual basis!" Dictatorial teachers appear to have little regard for individual circumstances: "If I give one student a break, then I have to give all students a break."

Enforcers like to subscribe to the "hot stove law," which states that any disciplinary action administered must be consistent with the consequences of a person touching a hot stove—the consequence is immediate, consistent, and impersonal. They believe that the classroom should show little tolerance for any misbehavior. The teacher places great value on order and control. The enforcer has little regard for concern for the individual student's personal problems. This style has characteristics of being autocratic, self-righteous, over-threatening, intimidating, and demeaning.

For example, if a student fails to bring in an assignment to school but has a very good excuse, this type of teacher would not accept any excuses and would give little time for listening to the student. Students soon learn that there is little flexibility in expected behavior and may develop fear and disrespect toward the teacher. The negative consequences for this type of style can vary. Students may become "yes students" in order to tolerate the threatening style. Students may find it difficult to become personal with this type of teacher and may feel that the classroom is somewhat like a prison.

The enforcer is one who imposes strict rules and creates a confining and controlling climate within the classroom. Students may feel "bottled up" and may not achieve as well because of their fear of asking questions to the teacher or their classmates. Moreover, a student may feel belittled or ridiculed by the enforcer to the point where the student may seek revenge. Students seek revenge by not coming to class, having a poor attitude, doing as little as possible, or doing something destructive to the school building.

Students also can feel that this type of teacher is unfair to them and can develop a great deal of stress and anxiety by being in the classroom. This anxiety can manifest itself through a lowering of self-esteem and lack of personal growth. When confronted by a principal about his/her discipline style, the enforcer can be very argumentive and condescending to a principal.

Abdicator

The "abdicator style" is characteristic of those teachers who are apathetic toward handling disciplinary problems and have little interest in their students. These teachers often feel "burned out" with the teaching profession and are awaiting retirement or another position. Abdicators tolerate a great deal of misbehavior in the classroom. They have low supporting and enforcing attributes.

Typical statements by the abdicator include: "If they want to sleep, I just let them sleep," "If they don't complete the work, I just flunk them—the heck with them," and "You can lead a horse to water, but you can't make it drink—if they come to class, fine; if they don't, it's their own problem." These teachers tend to avoid confrontation in addressing disciplinary problems.

Abdicators are often characteristic of the stereotypical teacher who has taught for many years and has become disgruntled with the profession. The abdicator tends to be somewhat reclusive, does little to motivate students, and does not care whether the students behave or not. Their classes tend to be disruptive. Abdicators would rather send their problem students to the school disciplinary dean than deal with the students themselves.

When students recognize this discipline style of teaching, they attempt to get away with as much as they can. Students will push the teacher to the limit with their misbehavior. They soon realize that the teacher has poor classroom management, and they, in turn, display little respect toward the teacher. This style of discipline can lead to student demotivation, poor academic achievement, and class disruption. The more aggressive students will take advantage of this type of teacher and will cause disruption for all students in the classroom. This type of teacher will exert the minimum amount of effort needed to manage students within the classroom. Not only do these teachers have a low regard for maintaining discipline, but this apathy will carry over to their attitude for student learning as well. The teachers tend to give little support to the students and will avoid negotiating with students unless they have to.

Like the enforcer, the abdicator can create havoc for the school administrators. It is difficult for the principal to effectively deal with the abdicator, especially if this teacher is protected by tenure. While the abdicator may do only the minimum effort required for teachers, his/her style of discipline may not be serious enough to warrant discharge.

Compromiser

The teacher who has a "compromiser" discipline style is one who tends to engage in a great deal of give-and-take bargaining with his/her students. The compromiser teacher appears to be more willing to compromise his/her own position than those of the students. Therefore, these teachers can be somewhat wishy-washy and inconsistent in enforcing school discipline policies. Examples of typical statements by the compromiser include, "Dealing with students is a give-and-take process; otherwise, they'll shut down on you and you'll get nowhere with them," and "I guess I find myself working with the student and compromising all the time." The compromiser teacher displays moderate assertiveness and empathy toward students. They tend to be inconsistent in enforcing policies and come across to students as manipulative and confusing. At times, they may have more concern with empathizing with students, while at other times they may embrace a more assertive discipline style. They place a high value on balancing the necessity of maintaining classroom discipline through a moderate degree of supporting students and enforcing policies.

There can be many negative consequences of this type of style. Students often become confused and do not know where they stand in dealing with the compromiser. Given the teacher's inconsistency in managing behavior, the teacher is often viewed by the student as a "wheeler dealer." Students often become frustrated with seeking a balance between their own behavior and the expectations of the teacher. As a result, this style often creates conflict among the students. Students may feel pitted against other students and develop resentment among their classmates because of this inconsistency in the enforcement of rules. They may believe some students receive less disciplinary action than themselves for the same type of offense.

Supporter

The "supporter" style teacher makes great efforts to talk with students about a disciplinary problem and will leave a great deal of latitude in the disciplinary action they may administer. This teacher places a high degree of empathy and concern for the student but shows little assertiveness. This teacher is very concerned about the personal feelings of the student and has a difficult time enforcing policies.

Typical statements of the supporter include: "I listen to my students, and if there are extenuating circumstances, I'll give them a break," and "I have a deep concern for the feelings of my kids and do my best to work with them—every kid is different and you can't treat them all the same." The supporter often takes a soothing and unassertive approach to handling discipline problems. They tend to give the students the benefit of the doubt and are often evasive and uncommitted to enforcing disciplinary action against a student for an offense.

The negative consequences of this style are that students will often run over the teacher and can get away with a great deal of misbehavior. The classroom will typically be disruptive, since the teacher typically places the needs of students over the need for rules and regulations. These teachers are concerned with insuring that the students are very comfortable and that there is an atmosphere of great care for students versus the need for insuring high performance and academic achievement. This type of teacher will sacrifice student learning for personal attention and feelings of the student.

Negotiator

The "negotiator" is a teacher who places great value on a win-win approach to disciplining students. These teachers have a high degree of both enforcing and supporting teaching styles. They strive to develop a learning environment where students will excel to their full potential. They demonstrate a balance of empathy and assertiveness with their students. These teachers make use of many approaches to discipline such as parent/teacher conferences, listening to students, enforcing rules and policies, telephone discussions with parents, and counseling sessions with their students.

The negotiator places high value on giving extra time after school to talk with students and parents in an effort to maintain a collaborative win-win environment. These teachers make statements such as, "Working with the student involves a collective process of parents, teachers, and the student coming to a consensus as to what is best for the student," and "I try to take an objective approach in counseling my students in finding suitable corrective action."

The negotiator is objective, committed, responsible, and takes charge in maintaining discipline in the classroom. They do not subscribe to a zero tolerance policy but recognize that all situations may warrant different disciplinary actions because of external circumstances. Negotiators investigate the facts of a given disciplinary situation prior to administering discipline. While these teachers value assertiveness in maintaining control, they also do this with love and respect toward their students.

There are few negative consequences of the negotiator teaching style. These teachers have a high degree of commitment to maintaining discipline without belittling and intimidating students. They also attempt to be consistent as much as possible while recognizing individual situations for offenses. The negotiator style is not one of a compromiser but, rather, one of collaboration.

Students respect this type of teacher, since they know the teacher enforces rules and regulations for the benefit of the entire school and that these teachers have a great deal of empathy for all students. The negotiator teachers tend to develop an attitude of "common stake" in the classroom through trust, respect, and mutual concern among everyone. They expect students to treat them with respect, and they respect their students as well. While the negotiator places a high value on rules and regulations, they place a higher value on student growth, flexibility, and appropriate freedom in the classroom.

The negotiator understands that at times he/she needs to emphasize enforcing or supporting attributes. For example, in times of life-threatening or other serious situations, the negotiator may act very assertively and enact enforcement for the best interests of the students and the school. At other times, in the case of a disabled student, the negotiator may act very supportively with little need for assertiveness. The negotiator uses the best disciplinary approach given his/her students, his/her own style, and the situation.

CHAPTER 5

Negotiating Mutual Agreement

BARRIERS TO EFFECTIVE DISCIPLINE

THE QUESTION OF whether to manage discipline is not an option for the teacher. The teacher must learn to manage discipline, or discipline will manage the teacher. A teacher can either have a positive or negative view toward discipline. Effective teachers have a positive view and learn to effectively manage disciplinary problems in their classrooms. Ineffective teachers develop a negative attitude toward discipline, which often leads to overall poor teaching, apathy, and burnout. Some of the barriers that can hinder a teacher from developing a positive attitude toward discipline are:

Overgeneralization

Some teachers perceive the disciplinary problems of students as a never-ending negative event with an underlying pattern of defeat. Typical statements might include, "These students always cause problems," or "If it weren't for the students, this would be a good job." The use of overgeneralization can have a negative impact and create a distorted view by viewing all students as troublemakers when, in fact, only a few may actually be the problem. Teachers generally know who their problem students are, and they shouldn't become disconcerted about teaching because of only a few students.

I Don't Negotiate with Students

Teachers who claim they do not negotiate with their students are only fooling themselves. In reality, every interaction a teacher has with a student can be considered negotiation. Even the highly authoritarian teacher who takes an assertive position still negotiates with students.

59

Authoritative teachers may give a student no option but to use aggressive tactics and strategies to counter the teacher's authoritative approach. A collaborative process of mutual respect between teachers and students entails effective interpersonal relations, respect, and negotiations.

Overpersonalization

For teachers, dealing with difficult disciplinary problems in a classroom can be personally overwhelming. Many teachers internalize these problems and overpersonalize students' misbehavior, which creates enormous internal stress. As a coping mechanism, teachers may develop an attitude of disrespect to all students, and overall dissatisfaction with teaching.

It is important for a teacher to recognize that the role of a teacher, like many professions, involves a certain need to distance oneself from the interaction. For example, if a medical doctor, who is working in an emergency room, personally internalizes the trauma of his/her patients onto himself/herself, this would negatively impact effective treatment. Likewise, a teacher needs to understand that students are not adults and do not have the same maturity level and that the role of the teacher includes being a disciplinarian.

Poor Time Management

A teacher who has properly planned and prepared for a day's activities will have fewer disciplinary problems in the classroom. Students are very keen at picking up when a teacher is disorganized; and in that moment of confusion, a class can get out of control. Likewise, the final five minutes of class time can be disastrous for the unorganized teacher since this is when discipline problems often erupt.

Ineffective Classroom Management

Experienced teachers realize the importance of the layout of a classroom. Teachers who plan the layout of a room so that it is optimum for the learning environment will have fewer discipline problems. Desks that are too close to each student or students who are positioned with other troublemakers can only be an invitation for problems.

Viewing Discipline as Magic

Establishing an effective discipline approach is not magic; rather, it is based upon a solid discipline philosophy, and realistic rules and behavioral expectations. Expecting students to act like adults is unrealistic.

Failure to Forgive Student Misbehavior

Teachers need to recognize that students will make mistakes and misbehave from time to time. The need to forgive students for misbehavior and to build upon their strengths is critical to motivating students and developing their self-esteem.

Organizational Instability

Nothing can be more difficult than for a teacher to establish a healthy learning environment when there are many distractions and instability within the organization of the school. Organizational problems can include poor leadership, union-board labor problems, conflict among teachers and administrators, low morale, poor communication, and overall disorganization. Expecting a teacher to focus on teaching while in a dysfunctional organization is unrealistic. The need to establish a positive school organization is essential for maintaining an effective discipline program.

Unrealistic Expectations

Teachers who place unrealistic expectations on student behavior and academic achievement create possible disciplinary problems. A teacher needs to establish high expectations; however, they must be realistic, flexible, and within reach for the students.

Inability to Say No

Many teachers have a difficult time saying "no" to their students. Teachers who try to overly accommodate the needs of their students invite discipline problems. Students tend to exploit teachers in these situations. This desire to accommodate students must be balanced with a realistic sense of judgment.

Lack of Skills

The experienced teacher who is able to manage disciplinary problems has a wide range of techniques in his/her arsenal. Information is power; the more a teacher understands about managing discipline, the more effective he/she will be. Students' needs are always changing depending upon their home and social environment, and the teacher needs to be aware of fads and values in order to maintain rapport with their students.

Distorted Thinking

Some teachers overreact and develop an "all or nothing" view toward their students. If a student's performance is poor, the teacher might be tempted to see the student as a loser. This distorted thinking can create a prejudice against all students and hinder the students' ability to behave.

Mind Reading

Teachers who attempt to read the minds of students and predict their behavior may feel they have good intuition; however, this practice can lead to disaster. While there may be some value in utilizing one's intuition about behavior, the teacher should always maintain an open perspective and avoid jumping to conclusions about the motives of a student.

The Halo Effect

The tendency for a teacher to develop early impressions of a student and then subsequently perceive and treat the student a certain way based upon these first impressions is called the "halo effect." The teacher can view a student as either doing no good or no wrong, depending upon whether the initial impression was positive or negative. Labeling a student as a behavior problem can be damaging to the attempt to improve the student's behavior. The teacher should resist the tendency to label students, especially with such labels as emotionally disturbed, mentally dysfunctional, or behaviorally impaired. While students may have legitimate mental and physical disabilities, by mislabeling and making presumptions a teacher can directly impact the student's behavior in the classroom.

Eliminating the Positives

After many years of teaching, even the seasoned teacher can become burned out with the profession and develop apathy toward teaching. Likewise, the new teacher may feel overwhelmed with the profession and develop a similar attitude. When faced with burnout, teachers may be prone to discount the positive and accentuate the negative. When teachers concentrate on the negative aspects of the job, burnout is magnified. Teachers need to appreciate and concentrate on the positive aspects of the job rather than dwelling on the negatives.

ESTABLISHING INTERPERSONAL COMMUNICATIONS

Managing student discipline requires the use of effective interpersonal communication skills. The ability to talk with a student and reach agreement so that both parties feel mutually satisfied is an ideal goal. Basic to the communication process is the need to establish meaningful two-way communication. When people utilize one-way communication, such as when a teacher does all the talking to the student, communication often breaks down. Therefore, the need to provide two-way communication between both parties (i.e., teacher and student) is important in resolving disciplinary problems.

Communication can be viewed as the process of formulating information and encoding this information, transmitting the information to the receiver, decoding the information, and then providing feedback to the original transmitter (see Figure 5.1). Feedback is important because it establishes and determines the quality of communication. This process can often occur almost instantaneously on a continuous basis between two people.

Several barriers can impact the quality of communication. For example, the period of time when a teacher decides to talk to a student (i.e., timing of information), the environment in which the conversation takes place, the personal approach utilized, the method or medium used, and

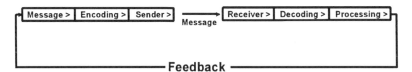

Figure 5.1. Communication model.

the actual selection of words and content all play an important part in the process.

For example, if a student is emotionally upset and an issue arises in front of the student's peers in the classroom, the teacher should select another time in which to confront the situation rather than at that moment. Confronting the issue in this volatile situation may escalate the matter. The teacher may decide that the best time to address the problem might be after class when they can be alone and the student has had time to calm down.

The environment plays an important part in the communication process. If a student is requested to discuss a discipline matter in a formal office, a higher degree of stress and sense of importance will be established rather than selecting a more neutral location such as a hallway or cafeteria. If a teacher would like to address a discipline problem on a more informal basis, it may be more effective to select a more neutral location. The medium that is used (i.e., method of communication) such as whether a teacher uses a letter, one-on-one verbal discussion, telephone, or another person, affects the communication outcome. These considerations should be taken into account by a teacher in deciding upon the best communication approach to use in communicating with students about disciplinary matters.

Listening is another element of the communication process. Without active listening on the part of both the teacher and student, the communication process will be hindered. The teacher must insure that he/she is genuinely listening to the student's position and must also insure that the student is listening as well. Most people speak around 150 words per minute, although they are able to listen up to between 400 to 600 words per minute. With this in mind, a listener's mind tends to wander, and he/she begins to think about other things while listening to a speaker. It is important that both parties pay close attention to each other. For example, the teacher may request a student's full attention before initiating a discussion.

There are many barriers to effective listening such as interrupting the other speaker, never looking at the other person when listening or talking, not allowing the other person a chance to talk, continually fidgeting with a pencil or object, pacing back and forth impatiently, staring at the other person, continuing to wander off the subject, attempting to finish the other person's sentences, arguing with every point, or answering a question with a question. Poor listeners also may prejudge other individuals, daydream while listening, become bored, look uninterested, and forget the information in the discussion. Good listeners look for areas of mutual agreement, keep an open mind, listen wholeheartedly, stay awake, and generally process the information that is being communicated.

For example, when a teacher is dealing with a student, it might be easy for the teacher to harbor preconceived notions about a student, especially if the student has had problems before. A teacher might prejudge the student and develop a prejudice based upon these past experiences. The teacher may not genuinely listen to the student's point of view. The teacher may also have a tendency to abuse his/her authority. It is easier for a teacher to tell a student to be quiet and lecture to the student than it is to engage in a two-way communication. While at times, it is necessary to say a quick command to a student to eliminate a discipline problem, at other times a two-way discussion is essential. Therefore, the ability to discern when to use one-way versus two-way communication is a prerequisite for the teacher in managing a disciplinary matter.

The use of nonverbal communication is also an important element in discussing a disciplinary matter with a student. Many factors impact on nonverbal communication, such as proxemics, kinesics, and body language techniques.

Proxemics, which entails the principles and observations in the use of space as an extension of an individual's personality, can play a significant impact in resolving a disciplinary matter between a teacher and a student. Some of the elements that affect proxemics might include the arrangement of furniture, physical distance between teacher and student, size and shape of a room, and physical appearance.

For example, the distance between the teacher and student can impact on the interpersonal relations during the communication process. A distance of more than four feet between the student and teacher indicates an impersonal atmosphere. A more personal distance is generally about two to four feet between the two parties. A distance of less than two feet might create a very intimidating and hostile situation. While a teacher needs to consider these general proxemic parameters, cultural differences may change the distances.

The use of kinesics involves the study of body movements—postures, facial expressions, and gestures. Teachers who exhibit power may use stern gestures and direct eye contact. A more collaborative approach includes a relaxed posture, positive facial expressions, and open body gestures. While some teachers may feel it is important to exhibit intimidating body language, this may have a negative impact on resolving a disciplinary matter since students may remain silent. The teacher should also be aware of exhibiting defensive body language signals, such as darting or glancing side-to-side, crossing one's arms in a rigid manner, or tensing body motions that can distract the student from discussing the disciplinary problem.

There are also differences in nonverbal communication that exist between people of different cultures. For example, a Hispanic student may not look a teacher in the eyes when being disciplined. While the teacher might view the student's downcast eyes as disrespectful, this nonverbal gesture may be normal for the Hispanic student. Recognizing differences in body language in a multicultural classroom is critical for teachers when disciplining students.

There are several communication techniques that can be utilized when talking with a student. For example, a teacher might utilize the technique of "paraphrasing." Paraphrasing means to repeat back to the student in the teacher's own words what the student said. This helps to reinforce the point that the teacher is listening to the student and insure that the message was understood. The use of "restatement" is a technique that can be used. Restatement means that the teacher repeats the student's statement verbatim back to the student in an effort to encourage the student to continue talking.

The teacher can use the techniques of open-ended and closed-ended questions. Open-ended questions cannot be answered by a simple yes or no and encourage the student to continue talking. Open-ended questions usually involve words such as who, what, where, when, and how. The use of open-ended questions encourages additional facts and information. Closed-ended questions can be effectively used when the teacher simply wants to obtain a yes or no answer. A simple phrase can yield a great deal of information and expedite the discussion.

Silence can be a powerful tool when talking between two parties. Often when faced with silence, individual students will talk. Using moments of silence in a skillful manner by the teacher can be a very valuable tool for opening up discussion and receiving more information from the student. Silence can also demonstrate that teachers are generally willing to listen to the student's concern.

The use of "expanders" is another technique of stating simple comments such as "Go on," "I understand," "I see." Expanders encourage the student to continue talking and have a reinforcing effect in establishing a mutual dialogue. A final technique includes eliminating distractions within the room. A noisy environment hinders effective discussion. Finding a more suitable environment is critical to disciplining a student.

UNDERSTANDING COMMUNICATION STYLES

An important factor that impacts upon the effectiveness of communication is the dominant communication style of people. Miscommunication often occurs when there is a difference in the communication styles between a teacher and student. The basis of communication styles was formulated by Carl Jung, a renowned psychoanalyst and student of Sigmund Freud. As an outgrowth of Jung's work on personality, four primary communication styles can be identified—the "intuitor," "feeler," "thinker," and "doer."

While each of us have and use all four styles, we tend to use one dominant style. The intuitor talks from a conceptional viewpoint and tends to communicate in the timeframe of the future. This person places an emphasis on creativity and originality. Intuitors often are wordy, ramble in their thoughts, and may be unrealistic and dogmatic. They look for unique and novel approaches to solve problems, but tend to be unrealistic. When placed in stressful situations, they can be egocentric, condescending, and unorganized.

The feeler communication style is one that values the feelings of other people. Feelers are good listeners and observers. To them, the feelings of people can often be more important than the results. They tend to be perceptive, patient, warm, and empathetic. Although they are people-oriented, they can be impulsive, moody, overdramatic, and overly emotional. They also tend to operate out of the timeframe of the past. While the communication style of a feeler has many positive attributes, feelers can be overemotional in a discipline situation. If a teacher has a predominant feeler style, he/she may overdramatize a student's problem. Likewise, a student who has a feeler style may more easily break down into tears.

The thinker communication style is objective, rational, and analytical. Thinkers can be effective in organizing thoughts and presenting them in a clear and logical manner. They can, however, be overcautious, rigid, and controlling. They tend to be indecisive in solving problems and would prefer to ponder rather than make a quick decision. Thinkers view things with respect to the past, present, and future timeframes. Thinkers can come across as being too rigid given their desire to follow a structured, point-by-point format. They may be criticized as being overly detailed, long-winded, legalistic, and businesslike.

The doer communication style is pragmatic and result-oriented. Doers act in the timeframe of the present. They are hard-driving and assertive.

They can be, however, too short-term oriented in their thinking and may forget long-term considerations. They tend to be combative, act quickly, and sometimes impulsively. The doer tends to be more concerned with the bottom line and communicates in a short and to-the-point manner. They are less likely to engage in personal and collaborative discussions with students and are more concerned with railroading their opinions.

The implications of communication styles are critical when dealing with disciplinary problems between a teacher and student. People with similar styles tend to communicate more effectively with each other. They tend to "talk the language" of the other party. However, if both parties overuse their style, conflict can arise. For example, if two doers are talking, they may both become too forceful and insensitive to each other. Likewise, two intuitors may become too conceptual and arrogant with each other and avoid confronting the disciplinary issue. The greatest weakness of a teacher in disciplining a student is often overusing their strength (i.e., their dominant communication style).

Problems in communication can arise when dealing with students who have a different style than the teacher. For example, if a teacher tends to be a doer and he/she is disciplining a student who is predominantly a feeler, the teacher may appear to the student as being overly assertive and lacking sensitivity. This situation can be overwhelming for the student, and the student may not listen or respond. The student may view the teacher as intentionally belittling him/her and disregarding him/her as a human being. On the other hand, if the teacher has a thinker communication style and the student has a doer style, conflict may arise. The teacher may be viewed as too controlling, nitpicky, and impersonal. The student may become frustrated and impatient and simply want to resolve the matter versus having an indepth and detailed discussion. The teacher may be viewed as too structured and overly cautious and conservative.

The key to communicating effectively with a student begins by identifying the teacher's own dominant style, then the style of the student. This does not mean that the teacher must permanently change but rather must adapt his/her approach for the student. For example, if the teacher is dealing with a student who is dominantly a feeler, the teacher should take extra time to personalize the discussion and be concerned with the student's feelings and emotions.

When approaching an intuitor, the teacher should be more dynamic and offer more creative and thought-provoking ideas. When dealing with a thinker, the teacher should structure the discussion in an organized and step-by-step approach. The thinker may also need more time to contemplate and process the discussion as compared to the doer who may be more inclined to quickly assess the bottom line. Teachers should get to the point with doers. However, it may be necessary to make sure the doer understands the details of the discussion when necessary.

Communication styles, like learning styles, can have a dramatic impact on the teacher's ability to resolve disciplinary problems. Recognizing and utilizing communication styles as a means to resolve disciplinary problems can be very effective in resolving day-to-day discipline problems.

CONDUCTING A COUNSELING OR DISCIPLINARY SESSION

The ability to effectively conduct a counseling or disciplinary session with a student is a fundamental requirement of all teachers. While teachers can at times nip disciplinary problems in the bud and resolve a matter quickly, quite often the teacher is faced with the need to sit down with the student and discuss the matter (see Figure 5.2).

Described below is an explanation of the steps in conducting a counseling or disciplinary session:

(*1*) Step 1: Describe the expected behavior. The teacher should begin the session by humanizing the setting, being objective, but firm in terms of describing the expected behavior required of all students within the school. The teacher might cite the school policy handbook to reinforce his/her position. Too often teachers are quick to blame a student for a disciplinary offense without first describing the school's policies and expectations for student behavior. By stating the expected behavioral standard, the teacher legitimizes the session.

(*2*) Step 2: State the misbehavior/offense. The teacher then should describe the student's alleged misbehavior/offense in a neutral, but firm manner and the discrepancy with the school policy. The teacher should give specific examples and actual facts to support the allegation. Any documentation, as well as statements by witnesses, can be helpful in collaborating the problem. During this step, the teacher should be careful not to personally belittle or degrade the student and create immediate conflict or friction between teacher and student. Otherwise, communication will be hampered.

(*3*) Step 3: Ask the student for the cause. In step three, the teacher asks the student for the reason or cause of the misbehavior or performance

1. Describe the Expected Behavior
   * Humanize the setting
   * Be objective
   * Be specific
   * Be firm, but fair

2. State the Misbehavior/Offense
   * Give facts
   * Cite examples

3. Ask the Student for the Cause
   * Identify the root cause:

     1. Outside influences--gangs, home, etc.
     2. Aptitude problem
     3. Attitude or motivation
     4. Health problem
     5. Need for special assistance

4. Acknowledge Feelings and Paraphrase Remarks

5. State the Disciplinary Action

6. Ask for Solution to Resolve Problem

7. Discuss and Agree on Solution

8. Explain Future Consequences for Misbehavior

9. Support Student and Build Confidence

10. Thank the Student

Figure 5.2. Steps in conducting a counseling or disciplinary session.

discrepancy. It is important that the teacher consider possible causes such as outside influences—peer influence, gangs, home environment, aptitude, attitude, motivation, health, or special conditions that uniquely contribute to the situation (e.g., disability). Often, if the teacher considers these causes, there is a good chance that one of them will be the root cause of the student's problem. During this step, it is important that the student acknowledge his/her responsibility for his/her action(s) and identify the root cause of his/her behavior. The teacher can help in discussing the root cause by offering suggestions. It may be possible that there wasn't a reason (i.e., root cause) for the student's misbehavior and that the student simply misbehaved without thinking.

(4) Step 4: Acknowledge feelings and paraphrase remarks. Step four involves listening to the student and acknowledging the student's feelings. Whether a teacher agrees or not with the student, it is important that the teacher personalizes the situation by at least acknowledging how the student feels. The student might express remorse, anger, or hostility. The teacher can respond by stating, "I can understand how you would feel in a situation like this," or "I can see how someone would have these feelings in a situation like this." Recognizing the student's feelings helps to personalize the conversation and develop an atmosphere of caring and respect. Even for students perceived to be cold and calculating, the teacher may still recognize the student's feelings. The teacher should also paraphrase the student's comments to demonstrate that the teacher is listening and understood the message.

(5) Step 5: State disciplinary action. The fifth step entails the teacher stating the disciplinary action that is being given to the student for the offense. If the session is a counseling session and not a disciplinary session, the teacher disregards this step.

(6) Step 6: Ask for solution to resolve problem. In step six, the teacher should ask the student for a solution to the problem. For example, if the student is failing to complete homework assignments, the teacher may ask the student how the work will get done in the future. Asking the student allows him/her to take responsibility for his/her own behavior. During this step, the teacher may need to offer various options, if the student doesn't. In this way, the student and teacher can negotiate and collaboratively resolve the disciplinary matter.

(7) Step 7: Agree upon solution. If the student suggests an appropriate solution to the problem, and it is agreeable to the teacher, the teacher should give his/her concurrence in step seven. When a student suggests a solution to his/her problem, the student is going more apt to accept the solution and be responsible versus when a teacher proposes a solution. If the student's suggestion is unacceptable to the teacher, then further discussion is necessary. If the student is unwilling to consider any reasonable options, the teacher may find it necessary to impose his/her own solution.

(8) Step 8: Explain future consequences for misbehavior. Step eight requires that the teacher explain the consequences for continued

misbehavior or poor performance. It is important that once an agreement is made the student recognizes that there will be future consequences if the student does not improve. This is important for establishing a progressive disciplinary approach with students.

(9) Step 9: Support student and build confidence. Step nine involves building confidence of the student and reinforcing the teacher's belief in the student. If the teacher supports the student and verbally states this to the student, the student will be more apt to improve. While it may be difficult at times for teachers to state this support, teachers must attempt to restore a positive working relationship. The teacher should also use appropriate body language. The subtle non-verbal cues and signals that a student picks up regarding a teacher's feeling toward a student can be as powerful as verbal words.

(10) Step 10: Thank the student. The last step consists of thanking the student for attending the session. The teacher should reinforce the positive aspects of the student. If necessary, the teacher may also require the student to sign his/her signature to a discipline action form, and he/she might schedule a follow-up session with the student to assess the student's improvement. After the session, the teacher should document the results of the session by writing a summary of the meeting and filing the information.

IMPROVING YOUR NEGOTIATING POSITION

There are many methods that a teacher can utilize to improve his/her negotiating position. The first is recognizing that the ultimate goal of a teacher is to reach a collaborative solution to a disciplinary problem that both teacher and student accept. While every teacher may want to quickly and decisively end a disciplinary problem, taking a hard-line approach is not always the best solution.

When an assertive teacher states a command to a student, the student always has a choice whether to obey. Although a student may obey the command immediately, the student may harbor significant resentment, which can manifest itself later on. Most of the day-to-day disciplinary problems can be effectively dealt with by the "discipline by negotiation" approach. However, it must be realized that in very serious situations where the safety of a student is a concern, a teacher must take aggressive action to resolve the matter. Even in very serious situations, however, a negotiating element may be present.

The objective of negotiation is to obtain a collaborative agreement in which both parties are satisfied. They do not feel that the negotiation element is a contest of will, that participants are adversaries, or that the goal of negotiation is to demand concessions and make threats. A teacher can increase his/her effectiveness as a negotiator by employing basic principles.

Commitment

Teachers must be totally committed to the learning environment to achieve positive discipline in the classroom. Teachers who have a commitment to their students will be more effective in handling disciplinary problems. The teacher who is uncommitted will be limited in his/her effectiveness.

Collaboration

Teachers who take a position that the feelings and opinions of students are valued and that negotiation is a two-way street will ultimately be more effective in developing trust and respect from the student. A collaborative approach in dealing with students can increase the teacher's effectiveness.

Well-Defined School Policies

Nothing can undermine a teacher's effectiveness as much as having ill-defined school discipline policies. The school discipline policies should be very clear, understandable, and fair and all students should be informed of the policies.

Consistent Policy Administration

School policies need to be enforced in a consistent manner. While extenuating circumstances should always be considered in a student disciplinary offense, the administration should attempt to be as fair and consistent as possible so that all students will respect the school policies and not feel there is prejudice and bias.

Skill Development

Teachers who continually develop their skills in handling disciplinary problems will be more effective in handling disciplinary problems. The values and interests of students are constantly changing, and the ability to deal with students is important. The ability of a teacher to handle different cultures and diverse populations that may have unique discipline problems is critical for the student. Conducting in-service programs and other staff development activities can improve a teacher's effectiveness and skill.

High Priority

Teachers who believe discipline is a high priority will be more effective. Handling discipline problems can mean a great deal of time beyond the classroom. Teachers may need to make parental telephone calls after school, meet with students, conduct parent disciplinary sessions, write letters, etc. The importance of spending time after class hours can contribute to fewer disciplinary problems within the classroom.

High Aspiration Level

Teachers who have a high aspiration for student achievement and behavior in the classroom will be more effective disciplinarians. Teachers who do not place much emphasis on student behavior will experience more problems. Students are very quick to recognize teachers who believe discipline is a serious matter versus those who don't.

Decisiveness

Teachers who deal with disciplinary problems decisively will be more effective in the classroom. Letting students misbehave or postponing addressing a disciplinary problem can only lead to more serious problems in a classroom.

CHAPTER 6

Creating a Win-Win Organization

BARRIERS TO SOLVING ORGANIZATIONAL PROBLEMS

DISCIPLINARY PROBLEMS IN a school may be symptomatic of underlying organizational problems. A school that has problems such as low staff morale, an unsafe environment, inadequate policies, poor leadership, ineffective communications, poor facilities, and inadequate instruction and curriculum will undoubtedly experience many disciplinary problems. It is difficult for teachers to concentrate on the learning process and managing student behavior when they are preoccupied by the school organizational problems. The ability of educators (i.e., teachers and administrators) to effectively diagnose an organization, find the root cause(s) of problems, implement effective solutions, and resolve school problems is critical in creating a productive and prosperous school environment.

If an educator is experiencing widespread disciplinary problems, he/she must undertake a systematic problem-solving and decision-making process to identify the causes and resolve the problems. Barriers to problem solving include the following.

Making False Comparisons

Far too often educators make false comparisons when attempting to solve disciplinary problems. The causes of disciplinary problems at one school may be entirely different than at another school. There may be substantial differences in the socioeconomic conditions of the community, multicultural aspects, building facilities, and home environments of the students that impact on student misbehavior.

Avoiding Schoolwide Issues

A common mistake made by educators in solving a disciplinary prob-

75

lem is not confronting schoolwide issues. For example, there may be a tendency for a teacher to avoid dealing with the problem of student absenteeism and truancy in his/her classroom, given that the problem may be a schoolwide issue that needs to be addressed at the administrator or district level.

Taking Action without Identifying the Root Cause

One of the most frequent barriers to problem solving is when an educator takes action without first identifying the problem (i.e., educators attempting to solve a problem based upon a proposed solution). For example, teachers facing disciplinary problems might state "The solution to our problem is that we need more security officers," or "The solution to disciplinary problems is that we need more enforcement of policies by administration." Attempting to solve a disciplinary problem based on a proposed solution is futile, without first isolating the actual cause.

Failing to Anticipate Widespread Effects

When educators fail to anticipate the widespread effects of discipline, action can cause problems to escalate. For example, if a teacher fails to actually identify the reason for a student's misbehavior and is more concerned about obtaining immediate control, the other students may view the teacher as being unfair to the student and the entire classroom. A student who is reprimanded unfairly can cause all the students to become unmotivated. Teachers who are inconsistent in administering discipline may not see the effects of the whole situation (i.e., all the students) and can create long-term problems.

Failing to Collaborate

When teachers fail to collaborate in dealing with disciplinary problems, the organization may experience dysfunction. Effective teachers are those who are able to negotiate with their students and, when necessary, collaborate on resolving a problem. Students who take an active role in the disciplinary process are more apt to develop ownership and improve their behavior.

Failing to Recognize Hidden Agendas

Problems may be difficult to solve when an educator has a personal hidden agenda or is involved in a powerplay with another educator. A teacher may be fed up with a particular student and have a hidden agenda of attempting to remove the student from the classroom rather than considering the best interests of the student. The teacher may also be involved in a powerplay with the principal, and the student may end up being caught in between the two.

Egocentrism, Mind Blocks, and Self-Serving Interests

An educator may have difficulty solving a problem due to his/her own egocentrism, mind blocks, or self-serving interests. Educators may develop an attitude that they are always right and have difficulty admitting when they may be wrong. Educators should not let their egos get in the way of doing what is best for the students. Educators should also remain open-minded when dealing with disciplinary problems.

Treating the Symptom versus the Cause of the Problem

A major problem of teachers can be to treat the symptom versus the cause of the problem. The analogy of taking an aspirin for a headache instead of finding out the cause of the headache is similar to solving disciplinary problems. For example, a teacher may keep disciplining a student without ever finding out the reason for the student's problem.

Acting First and Thinking Later

A tendency for some teachers is to act first and think later. Too often the teacher is concerned with the lesson at hand and might quickly tell a student to be quiet because the teacher cannot afford to take the time to deal with the incident. Given that the teacher may be preoccupied with other activities, the tendency is to quickly stifle any misbehavior and then worry about it later. While this may be reality in dealing with the job of a teacher, if the teacher can take a few extra moments to think out the disciplinary situation, it may save a great deal of time later in dealing with its results.

STEPS IN SOLVING DISCIPLINARY PROBLEMS

There are many times when a teacher has a misbehaving student with whom he/she has difficulty identifying the cause of the problem. Nothing can be more frustrating for a teacher than to be unable to figure out the reason for the student misbehavior and resolve the problem. A teacher can view solving disciplinary problems as a systematic process of identifying the cause of the problem and taking the necessary actions (see Figure 6.1).

The steps to solving disciplinary problems are:

(*1*) Step 1: Conditional analysis. In step one, conditional analysis, the teacher should be concerned with analyzing the disciplinary situation. For example, if the teacher is experiencing a significant upsurge of disciplinary problems in the classroom, this first step entails examining the overall dynamics of the classroom such as the types of student offenses, when the offenses are being committed, who is primarily committing the offenses, and current disciplinary program.

Conditional analysis is similar to a medical doctor who first examines a patient by completing a history and physical report. The doctor records the patient's symptoms, past and present health

```
Step 1.    Conditional Analysis

Step 2.    Problem Definition

Step 3.    Fact Finding Investigation

Step 4.    Identify Most Likely Cause

Step 5.    List Possible Solutions

Step 6.    Analyze Each Solution

Step 7.    Select the Best Solution

Step 8.    Development of a Contingency Plan

Step 9.    Implement the Best Solution

Step 10.   Evaluate the Results of Solution
```

Figure 6.1. *Steps in solving disciplinary problems.*

problems, and medications being taken. Likewise, the teacher should collect all the relevant information in order to make an accurate "diagnosis."

(2) Step 2: Problem definition. In step two, the teacher starts the problem-solving phase of the process. The teacher writes the definition of the problem. For example, the teacher may define the problem as "a recent increase in student talking without permission during the beginning of the class period." This process helps the teacher clearly define the problem in need of resolution.

(3) Step 3: Fact finding investigation. Step three entails the educator investigating the facts surrounding the disciplinary problem. In this stage, the educator should look at the "who, what, where, and when." The educator should examine any deviations from what has normally been experienced in the past. For example, the teacher may identify increased incidents of fighting between female students in the cafeteria at lunch time. The educator should identify the "what is" versus the "what is not." For example, the "what is" could be identified as predominantly freshman and sophomore girls who are fighting versus junior and senior girls (the "what is not"). In this manner, the educator is able to dissect the problem by pinpointing the actual facts to the disciplinary situation.

(4) Step 4: Identifying most likely cause. In step four, the educator actually completes the problem-solving phase of the process by identifying the most likely cause for the disciplinary problem. There may also be more than one cause of the problem, in which case, the educator should write down the actual causes and rank them in terms of their priority.

(5) Step 5: List of possible solutions. After identifying the most likely cause, the educator begins the decision-making phase by listing the various solutions for resolving the disciplinary problem. Solutions might consist of separating problem students from one and another, revising the school policy, training teachers in the administration of the policies, making curriculum and instruction changes, or other organizational improvements.

(6) Step 6: Analysis of each solution. In step six, the merits of each solution should be examined for their strengths and weaknesses in resolving the disciplinary problem. For example, if the disciplinary problem is an increase in student assaults, the educator may work with a committee in examining possible solutions such as educating students about assaults, or making building improvements (e.g.,

additional lights, structural remodeling, restricting students to a specific area, or adding security officers).

(7) Step 7: Selection of the best solution. Step seven concludes the decision-making phase by the educator selecting the best solution in resolving the problem. For example, the solution may be to remove a problem student from the classroom and place him/her in an alternative school, change the school disciplinary policies, or improve the school curriculum and instruction. The selection may also involve choosing more than one solution for the problem.

(8) Step 8: Development of a contingency plan. Step eight involves developing a contingency plan should the implementation of the solution not be effective. For example, if the problem is student assaults, contingency plans might include harsher penalties to offenders, more elaborate building changes, or increased security officers.

(9) Step 9: Implement the best solution. In step 9, the best solution is implemented. The process should include good communications and collaborative involvement when possible.

(10) Step 10: Evaluate the results of solution. After implementing the solution, the last step involves conducting an evaluation of the results. Once an evaluation has been made continuous improvements can be made.

CREATING ORGANIZATIONAL CHANGE

A school that has widespread discipline problems requires a systematic organizational assessment and change effort. While educational leaders have utilized various organizational change models, these models have often fallen short of expectations in providing meaningful school change. Organizational-wide school change requires the involvement of all stakeholders (e.g., teachers, administrators, students, board members, parents, and community members).

Implementing school change can be viewed as a five-step process of planning, assessing, executing, implementing, and evaluating. Each phase entails a comprehensive process in working with all stakeholders of the school in bringing about meaningful change within the organization.

Step 1: Planning

This first phase, planning, begins with the principal working with a steering committee made up of various stakeholder representatives such as a teacher, administrator, board member, parent, union representative, and community member. The purpose of this committee is to develop the change plan and provide inspiration and direction for the school, overcome roadblocks, and provide resource support (e.g., finances, materials, facilities, and time).

The first goal of this phase is to develop a clear vision statement that reflects the needs of the students. This vision statement should represent a crystallized long-range picture of what should be accomplished at the school. The vision statement becomes the foundation for the ongoing process and helps to maintain a central focus while making educational decisions.

After the vision statement had been established, the steering committee should develop this statement into a school improvement plan (SIP), which includes such things as general mission statements, organizational goals that are aligned with district, and state goals and outcomes. Once the SIP is complete, the committee should insure that everyone understands the change plan by conducting "awareness sessions." This communication effort is a critical component in ensuring that everyone understands the collaborative process, expectations, and their roles in accomplishing the goals and objectives.

Step 2: Assessing

The purpose of step two, assessing, is to clearly identify the organization's strengths and areas in need of improvement (i.e., the major educational problems and concerns faced by the school). Assessment areas might include curriculum and instruction, safety and security, communications, morale, technology, student transportation, facilities and resources, student-centeredness programs and activities, work responsibilities, leadership and staff development, and parent and community involvement. This information can be collected through the use of organizational surveys or employee interviews in conjunction with an analysis of student test scores, attendance and other student data.

Once the assessment information has been analyzed, a report should be written outlining the organization's strengths and areas in need of improvement. Feedback sessions should be held for all stakeholders whereby the organizational strengths and areas in need of improvement can be debriefed. Feedback sessions allow everyone to understand the assessment information, clarify issues, and to ask questions about the process.

Step 3: Executing

To address areas in need of improvement, quality teams consisting of stakeholder representatives can be formed to work on the organizational issues. Quality teams might consist of multiculturalism, facilities, security, student achievement, discipline, parent and community relations, and technology. All team members should be trained in team building and group facilitation to ensure effective meeting management.

Quality teams should also consist of stakeholders who genuinely desire to work on school improvement issues or are associated with the defined issue by nature of their work responsibilities. For example, if the issue is to improve discipline, the school disciplinary dean should be involved on this quality team. A listing of each team and issue can also be posted on a bulletin board where interested participants can sign up. Some general guidelines for the quality teams might include voluntary membership, ground rules for conducting the meetings, and clear work goals.

Each quality team should be led by a facilitator. The role of the facilitator should be communicated to all members. The facilitators should also keep the quality teams on task, develop meeting agendas and minutes, and act as a communication link with the steering committee and stakeholders.

Benchmarking initiatives (i.e., a process in which the best practices of other schools are identified) can also be undertaken as a basis for achieving greater performance. Benchmarking teams can be established and can work with the quality teams, or the quality teams can develop sub-teams which can conduct the benchmarking.

Step 4: Implementing

Upon approval by the steering committee, the action plans should be implemented. The quality teams do not necessarily have to be responsible for actually implementing the action plans. For example, the discipline team might develop a new discipline program, but the disciplinary dean might actually implement it.

The quality team can stay "on the sidelines," and monitor the progress, act as a liasion with the steering committee, assist the dean, and help manage the process. Examples of quality team actions include extending school days to raise student test scores, improving school facilities, and developing the school curriculum, instruction, or policy changes.

Step 5: Evaluating

Upon implementation of the action plans, the quality teams should work with appropriate stakeholders in evaluating the results of the actions. Follow-up surveys, individual and group interviews, student academic assessment, and benchmarking comparisons can all be a part of the process. The teams can be rewarded for their efforts and achievements through various intrinsic rewards systems such as t-shirts, buttons, certificates, and luncheons.

When the student performance is increased, the students should be recognized. Recognizing students and including parents and the community in publicized school events can result in personal satisfaction and motivation for continued success.

Variations of this process can easily be adapted for an organization based upon its unique needs and characteristics. While this five-step process can be useful when conducted in conjunction with a school improvement plan, it can also be valuable as an intervention process at any point in the school year. If a school is suddenly put on probation, this process can be used to reassess the school and make necessary changes.

LEGAL ASPECTS OF DISCIPLINE

The ever-increasing complexity of state and federal laws and regulations concerning the disciplining of students can be overwhelming for any educator. School discipline policies must operate within existing laws. As these laws change over time, educators need to keep up to date with these changes. Any educator who has experienced a lawsuit well understands the emotional anxiety associated with defending it. Defending a lawsuit can take a significant amount of school resources such as time, money, and people. The best policy is to practice "defensive discipline management" and to take steps to prevent litigation.

"Defensive discipline management" entails understanding and enforcing the legal requirements of all educators in disciplining students, the legal rights of students, and the rights of educators and the school. Some of the legal requirements expected of teachers include the prevention of teacher insubordination, incompetence, and criminal acts. A teacher may be found insubordinate when he/she fails to follow school policies regarding discipline policies or the direct orders of an administrator unless the life or safety of a person's life is at risk. For example, if a teacher is ordered to supervise a playground while students are present and willfully violates this responsibility and a student is involved in an incident that harms another student, the teacher and school may be liable.

Administrators must conduct regular performance evaluations of teachers and be responsible for a teacher's performance. If a teacher is found to be incompetent because of his/her failure to properly discipline students or perform his/her duties in a satisfactory manner and the principal tolerates this performance, then the principal may be held responsible.

The school must also protect against teachers who are involved in criminal acts, especially acts involving immorality, robbery, and use or sale of illegal drugs, in order to protect the welfare of students. Students have the right to be protected from teachers who are involved in such criminal acts.

Educators must also be aware of the guidelines regarding disciplining students with disabilities and remedies for unlawful disciplinary actions. Some general guidelines for maintaining an appropriate legal environment in disciplining students are:

Compensatory Damages

Schools may be liable for compensatory damages if injury is incurred by students due to unreasonable or inappropriate disciplinary action, such as excessive discipline, physical punishment, threat, coercion, or group punishment that causes harm to students.

Corporal Punishment

Schools that allow the administration of corporal punishment, if in violation of state or school board policy, may be held liable.

Student Safety

Schools may be held liable for the failure to provide reasonable care and guidelines for students while on school property and while off the school premises if the activity is related to school-related activities.

Due Process

Students must be guaranteed due process for disciplinary action of a very serious nature such as expulsion. Schools must take into account the appropriate disciplinary action for a given offense, taking into consideration characteristics of the student such as possible disability, prior discipline history, and school policies.

Discipline Policies

All schools should have clearly stated disciplinary policies, and these policies should be well communicated to all students and parents. School policies must be written in accordance with federal and state guidelines and should not be written as to be deemed unreasonable or excessive.

Reasonable Discipline Action

Reasonable disciplinary action should be given to students for a given disciplinary offense that does not disrupt the student's academic process unless well substantiated. Schools should restrain from administering group punishment for individual students who have committed a disciplinary offense.

Progressive Discipline

Schools should utilize a progressive disciplinary approach, which affords students due process for actions committed by students ranging from least severe to most severe. Schools should also consider mitigating and extenuating circumstances when deciding upon disciplinary action for a disciplinary offense. Students should be given due process and should not be summarily transferred to other schools for disciplinary offenses.

Teacher Responsibilities and Authority

One method to help insure that a school has an effective disciplinary policy is to clearly delineate the responsibilities of teachers and to give them the necessary authority in carrying out their role. The responsibility of teachers in insuring that students behave properly is grounded under the jurisdiction of the school.

While under the jurisdiction of the school, teachers are similar to parents, *in loco parentis* (in place of the parent). Therefore, it is necessary for teachers to have the responsibility and authority to properly insure that students behave according to the standards of the school. While teachers may have authority, they must not participate in arbitrary, capricious, or discriminatory acts against students.

In making decisions regarding disciplinary matters, teachers must always consider the circumstances of the students such as age, emotional stability, physical or mental disabilities, or grade level. Therefore, teachers must be well trained in handling disciplinary matters and be granted wide discretion in administering disciplinary actions against students based upon the circumstances.

Students with Disabilities

Students with disabilities have special rights and considerations when being disciplined. For example, a disabled student must be given a due process hearing prior to being suspended or expelled to determine whether the disciplinary offense was related to the student's disability.

If the school is warranted in expelling a disabled student, the school must provide the disabled student with an alternative educational setting. Moreover, states may have specific laws regarding the disciplining of disabled students. For example, one state supreme court ruled that schools are forbidden from excluding disabled students from school for more than ten days for disruptive conduct as a result of their disability (Illinois State Board of Education, 531F.SUPP.148).

Married or Pregnant Students

Schools have a responsibility to provide education for married or pregnant students. These students must not be excluded from being allowed to participate in extracurricular activities or other academic activities of the school. Therefore, a teacher may not discipline or take disciplinary action against a student because he/she feels a pregnant student has an immoral character.

Recent laws have also supported the notion that pregnant students may fall under the definition of a "disabled person." Likewise, various state and federal laws protect the rights of married students that participate in extracurricular activities. Students should also not be coerced or threatened by teachers for desiring to become married or pregnant (*Beeson v. Kiowa Schools RE-1,* 39 Colorado App.174, 1977).

Profanity and Vulgar Language

The Supreme Court has upheld the right of a school to develop appropriate policies for student conduct and to have the authority to discipline students for misbehavior involving vulgar or profane language. Schools should not tolerate any obscene, rude, or profane language or gestures. Any offensive language or gesture that does not demonstrate the proper respect toward the school or people can be a basis for disciplinary action. Inappropriate language or gestures can also agitate and incite other students to misbehave.

Writing and Distribution of Publications

Another type of an expression protected by the first amendment involves the right of freedom to distribute publications. However, similar to freedom of expression, schools have the authority to insure that the publications do not disrupt the educational process.

School authorities may also establish guidelines regarding the appropriate duration and distribution of literature by students while on school grounds. While students may be protected under the first amendment for expressing political views, this expression must not be done in a vulgar manner or in a manner which substantially interferes with the operation of the school. For example, students may have the right to print a student newspaper, but they do not have the right to make libelous statements, utilize obscene or indecent language, or encourage acts of violence against the school and people.

Student Use of School Facilities

School authorities have the responsibility to treat all people consistently. If religious and other organizations request the use of facilities, schools cannot bar any organizations unless the activity poses disruption to the school. Schools have the authority to establish policies on the use of the school facilities. For example, if schools decide against allowing religious organizations to use their facilities, they must apply the same policy to other organizations.

While schools have generally been restricted from requiring students to pray in public schools, the use of voluntary prayer has been less conclusive. Courts have allowed the use of school premises on a voluntary basis for religious prayer. The Federal Court has passed the Equal Access Act, which assures religious students the use of school premises during noneducational time for religious or political reasons. While the Equal Access Act gives authorization for the use of school facilities by religious and political organizations, it does not allow for any activity that may be deemed unlawful, disruptive to the school, or may cause violence within the school (Reutter, 1994).

Student Conduct While off School Premises

Schools have the responsibility for protecting students and insuring their safety in a reasonable manner. School authorities have the right to establish reasonable rules and guidelines regarding student behavior while off the school premises that impact on their conduct while at school. For example, schools can establish reasonable guidelines regarding student conduct while on a school bus en route to school or while walking to school with other students. A school may have partial liability if students are harmed by other students while en route to school.

Several state and federal cases (Reutter, 1994), have given authority to schools to enforce rules against student athletes for use of drugs and alcohol while off the school premises. School authorities can discipline students for inappropriate behavior while on school field trips and other activities off the school premises. The school has the authority to discipline students for vulgar language and activities directed at school personnel while in the presence of other students when off the school premises (*Kline v. Smith, 1986*).

Student Discipline and Search Procedures

The fourth amendment of the United States Constitution insures "the right of people to be secure in their persons, houses, papers, and effects from unreasonable searches and seizures." However, school authorities have the right to conduct searches of a student's locker if there is reasonable belief that there is a violation of a school policy.

For example, a blanket search of student lockers on a periodic basis in order to insure the safety and security of students is generally permissible. Students should be told of the periodic searches. If a teacher has reasonable cause that an odor emanating from a locker is from drugs, school authorities generally would have the right to inspect the locker. The search and seizure of a student's personal belongings, body, or backpacks generally are acceptable, but generally require higher standards for search and seizure.

The bodily search of a student or a student's car in the school parking lot requires a high standard of probable cause in order to prevent violation of a student's civil rights. Without significant probable cause, school authorities may be held liable for damages. School authorities must make search decisions based upon the necessity of insuring the general welfare of students and the educational process without excessively intruding upon the student's civil rights. When possible, it may be preferable to obtain a student's permission prior to a search. In other cases, the use of police officers and other security officials may be warranted.

Police officers may need to secure a valid warrant in order to search a student or remove a student from the school grounds. Whenever a student is questioned by police officers on school grounds, students should benefit from the same rights as other citizens. Parents should be notified of any serious disciplinary matters involving police officials.

If a student is suspended from school, the courts have generally not required the school to constitutionally protect the student in attending graduation ceremonies. The graduation ceremony tends to be viewed a symbolic result of education, not a requirement. However, if a student meets the requirements for graduation and is expelled or suspended, generally the diploma must be issued.

Student Rights and Gang Activities

The rights of students hinge upon the first and fourteenth amendments of the United States Constitution. These amendments guarantee students the certain rights of freedom of speech, liberty, and equal protection of the law. The schools, in essence, are agents of the state and are responsible for protecting the basic rights of students. While administrators must protect the rights and safe operation of the school, the individual rights of students must also be recognized.

Administrators must adopt a balance in protecting the rights of both the school and the students. The school must not overly enforce regulations that are deemed excessive to a student's individual rights. However, in some instances, a school may take severe action in adopting school policies in order to protect the safety of the students.

Some basic guidelines in reaching this balance include the importance of insuring that the action of any individual student will not cause a disruption to the educational process or that the actions of an individual student do not violate the rights of other students. The importance of utilizing a collaborative process involving the parents and community is essential in establishing disciplinary rules and policies for a school.

While there is controversy regarding establishing policies involving student dress, symbolic speech forms, freedom of the press, and use of facilities, educators can follow some general guidelines. The first amendment of the United States Constitution provides for freedom of speech. The rights of students for freedom of speech is protected unless their statements are libelous, obscene, or threatening, or if they disrupt the normal operation of the school and educational process. Freedom of speech includes symbolic speech, which consists of such items as slogans, clothing, pins and buttons, and other related bracelets and jewelry.

The issue of symbolic speech has seen considerable attention in recent years due to gang-related activities. Gangs and other ritualistic criminal activities (e.g., Satanism) pose a major threat to schools. These activities can create a major disturbance and disruption to the safety and welfare of students. In fact, according to the 1996 twenty-eighth annual Phi Delta Kappa/Gallup poll of public attitudes towards the public schools, the category of fighting, violence, and gangs was ranked number three as the biggest problems facing local schools, surpassed only by drug abuse and lack of discipline.

A large culture of gang activity involves the use of symbolic symbols. Various gangs such as the Vicelords, Disciples, Latin Kings, Hustlers, and Gangster Disciples utilize a variety of sophisticated symbolic messages and symbols. Hand signals are one of the more popular methods of communication and the most difficult for school officials to manage. The use of hand signals by gang members can communicate anything from gang identity, drug dealing, violence, potential assault, and death. Learning the various hand signals can be very valuable for school educators in preventive discipline problems.

Other common gang and satanic symbolic identifiers include earrings, hats, bracelets, gloves, specific types of athletic shoes, hair styles, type of clothes, friendship beads, shoe laces, jewelry, buttons, combs, and style of dress. For example, hats that are worn tilted to the right or left can designate a particular gang membership. Jewelry and buttons such as a five- or six-point star, rabbit head, necklace, emblem, and a t-shirt worn under a hat can be symbolic of gang identification and thereby possible discipline violation. Something as common as a pair of athletic shoes can communicate a variety of gang messages. The color of the shoes, types and colors of laces, position of laces, position of the tongues of the shoes, and how the shoe is laced can communicate specific gang affiliation and potential gang activities. The style and color of a student's hair can also be a symbol of gang affiliation such as a specific haircut design, haircolor streaking, use and position of ponytails, barrettes, and other types of hair combs and pitchforks. The type of dress by a student can indicate a gang affiliation, such as whether a student wears a specific type of sports cap, jacket, or style and type of dress.

A number of ritualistic criminal symbols (e.g., Satanism and devil worship) can be highly destructive to the educational process. Satanists commonly take vows of secrecy and identify with such deities as Satan, Lucifer, and the underworld Prince of Darkness. Students can be heavily influenced to participate in such ritualistic activities through association with drug dealers, peer pressure, certain lyrics of heavy metal music, and fantasy role playing such as Dungeons and Dragons, witchcraft, demonology, and black magic. Various ritualistic symbols might include emblems of a serpent, upside-down cross, pentagram, a star and moon combination, upside-down pentagram, baphomet, goat's head, hexagram, and various circles and triangles.

Educators need to address gang and ritualistic activities in order to insure the safety and sanity within schools. Educators need to become involved through such measures as becoming knowledgeable about these problems, offering appropriate guidance, being concerned for students as human beings, involving the family, developing appropriate school policies, taking immediate action, working with the local police and community, and establishing in-school task forces. While it must be remembered that the burden of proof rests upon the school to demonstrate how these activities disrupt the normal operation of school, educators must take aggressive action as they try to balance these actions while insuring the rights of students. Dress codes and other school policies may be warranted in insuring student safety.

CHAPTER 7

Discipline Negotiation Strategies

INEFFECTIVE NEGOTIATING PRACTICES

ONE OF THE best ways to promote good behavior in a classroom is to utilize principles of effective negotiation. How a teacher conducts himself/herself in the classroom can be one of the most powerful influences on student behavior. However, there are many ineffective negotiating practices that only serve to erode the classroom environment. They include:

Scolding

When teachers become stressed and insensitive to the feelings of students, they often scold their students. If scolded on a continuous basis, students will become immune to this practice and will "shut down." Students become disrespectful toward teachers who scold them. They also become apathetic and demotivated toward learning and school, and develop a lower self-esteem.

Writing Assignments

The use of writing assignments and other punitive measures to resolve misbehavior creates negative consequences. If the students are given writing assignments for their penalty for misbehavior, they may associate learning as punishment. Once the student associates punishment with writing, they may then be demotivated in learning further writing skills. Therefore, writing assignments can have a negative affect and should be avoided.

93

Sarcasm

Dealing with a constant disruptive student is unpleasant for any teacher. Over time, it is difficult for teachers to maintain their composure and avoid being sarcastic to the students. The use of sarcasm never resolves a disciplinary matter, but can only make it worse. When a teacher is sarcastic to a student, the student views this behavior by the teacher as a personal attack. The teacher's inappropriate behavior, in turn, allows the student to justify his/her own misbehavior. The effect of sarcasm leads to overall erosion of the classroom environment.

Lecturing to Students

Teachers should avoid lecturing to students about their misbehavior. Students generally will "tune out" the teacher who lectures to them. Lecturing creates negative feelings in a student. These negative feelings may be later manifested through their continued misbehavior or resentment towards the teacher and school. Lecturing also stifles two-way collaborative discussions in resolving disciplinary problems.

Humiliating Students

When possible, discipline should be a private matter between the student and teacher. Disciplining students in front of their peers can cause them to feel humiliated. Teachers should be careful not to talk to students in a manner that doesn't humiliate them, otherwise, collaborating with the student on a disciplinary problem will be difficult.

Administering Punitive Actions

Teachers should never use punitive acts that hinder motivation, such as using a student as a poor example and embarrassing the student in front of the class. Likewise, other students should not be singled out as an example of good behavior, which will only pit one student against another. Teachers should be careful not to give up on the chronic misbehavior. While it may easy to lose respect for the chronic misbehaviors, teachers need to continue to work with them.

Negative Body Language

The use of threatening body language can also speak more loudly than the words the teacher may use. The teacher should refrain from pointing a finger at a student and using intimidating posture. Likewise, the teacher should talk in a respectful and professional manner and avoid negative phrases and talking in a condescending tone of voice.

Playing Favorites

Teachers should also be careful not to play favorites among students since this practice will persecute other students. The teacher should always attempt to be consistent in discipline, while at the same time, take into account mitigating circumstances when disciplining a student.

NEGOTIATING WITH CHALLENGING STUDENTS

There are several types of challenging students who have specific distinguishing characteristics. Learning to identify them and developing specific skills in managing them can increase the teacher's chances in negotiating with students. Some of them include:

The Chronic Talker

Dealing with students who chronically talk without permission or those who dominate class discussions is one of the more frustrating disciplinary problems for a teacher. There can be many reasons for this behavior such as the need for personal attention, desire to irritate the teacher and/or classmates, or as a release for the student's hyperactivity. Some suggestions for negotiating with the chronic talker include:

(*1*) Class layout: Change the arrangement of the room by moving the student's desk closer to the teacher or away from other chronic talkers. The teacher may also ask the student to switch seats with another student or move the student to a remote spot in the room so that it makes it more difficult for the student to continue talking.

(2) Praise and positive reinforcement: For the student who dominates discussion, the teacher should not reinforce the behavior through

praise and other positive reinforcements. The teacher might paraphrase the student's comment and move on to other activities.

(3) Positive body language: A powerful negotiating tactic is the use of body language for the constant talker. Giving a direct stare at the student with rigid folded arms may send a signal to the student to be quiet. Also, walking in close proximity toward the student without stopping a lesson can be a convenient and creative method to control student misbehavior without the student losing face.

(4) Silence: When a student is talking without permission while the teacher is teaching, the teacher can pause for a moment, and the silence may get the attention of the student and cause the student to stop talking. The teacher can also effectively use silence in combination with nonverbal messages to bring attention to the student's problem.

(5) Name dropping: A simple, but effective technique for the chronic talker is to state the name of the student (i.e., name dropping) while lecturing and the student will often stop talking. In this way, the teacher can continue a lesson without needing to stop and disrupt the entire class for one talker. A danger in doing this, however, is that the entire class's attention is focused on the student, which may cause embarrassment to the student. Therefore, the teacher should not overly use this technique.

(6) Counseling session: Conducting a counseling session with a student can be a very effective means of dealing with the chronic talker. While many teachers resent taking so much time to counsel with a student for such a problem, the counseling session, nevertheless, can be an effective way of investing time in eliminating a problem and preventing it from escalating in the future.

The Profane Talker

The student who uses profanity when talking in class shows disrespect to everyone in the classroom. The use of profanity is not uncommon since many students are influenced to talk in this manner by movies, music, and their peers. Students seek peer approval, power, and acceptance through use of profanity and foul language. They may also use profanity to compensate for their difficulty in expressing themselves, especially when experiencing strong emotions. Some ideas in negotiating with profane talkers include:

(*1*) Class rules: Strict school policies and class rules need to be established and clearly communicated to the students. Managing foul language in the classroom can be tricky for a teacher given that the teacher needs to eliminate the problem without destroying the self-esteem of the student. Talking with a student about the use of profanity should be done with the student to help him/her understand the ill effects of using the language.

(*2*) Control emotions: The teacher should control his/her own emotions when dealing with a student who uses foul language. Teachers often may feel personally attacked and should not consider the use of the foul language as a personal affront, given that the language may be commonplace for the student. Therefore, the teacher should remain calm and controlled when dealing with the student. Teachers must "practice what they preach," and act as a positive role model for their students. Teachers will be much more effective in managing the students' behavior if their own behaviors are professional.

(*3*) Suggest alternatives: Suggest alternative words for the student to express himself/herself. Ask the student to think of other words that can be used in place of the obscenity.

(*4*) Confront the behavior: Never abdicate responsibility in addressing foul language. Given the context of the situation, the teacher may need to schedule a conference with the chronic student. The conference might consist of a disciplinary session, a phone call to the student's parents, or conference with the disciplinary dean.

The Hyperactive Student

Hyperactive students are commonplace in schools. Students who have difficulty sitting for long periods of time, settling down, stopping fidgeting, or moving about the room can be very disruptive for the entire class. While some student hyperactivity may be rooted in a medical problem, many children simply have a high degree of energy, and this behavior can be managed without medical intervention.

While research has been inconclusive, some research suggests a link between watching violent and aggressive behavior on television and a student's own behavior. Teachers should not be quick, however, to discount a medical problem with the student. Attention Deficit Disorder (ADD) is a common occurrence with students today. Research studies suggest that the percentage of ADD students may be as high as ten to fifteen percent and most of these ADD students experience hyperactivity (Goldstein, 1995). Ideas in negotiating with hyperactive students include:

(*1*) Reduce stimuli. A student's hyperactivity might be increased by too much classroom stimulation. Many students simply do not respond well in a high activity-based environment. The high degree of stimuli can be overpowering to the hyperactive student. Therefore, reducing class stimuli can help this situation.

Asking the hyperactive student to take a different seat in the classroom where there are fewer stimuli or trying to minimize overall distraction in the classroom can be effective. Students also may get preoccupied by looking out a window, a hallway, or other external locations, which may cause the student to become hyperactive. The student may be best suited when seated in front of the room close to the teacher. This position may allow the student to gain more attention and to be more effectively under the management of the teacher.

(2) Provide structure. The teacher may attempt to provide more structure and organization for the student. The teacher may tailor the student's work assignments or require more focused reading. The teacher may also encourage students to operate on a more consistent daily routine. A more formal instructional approach versus cooperative learning and other methods may be more suitable for the hyperactive student.

(3) Patience. Exercise patience with the hyperactive child and focus on good behavior. Praise the student for his/her good performance and behavior and use nonverbal cues to reinforce the student's appropriate behavior. For example, the teacher may give hand signals to the student illustrating that the student should lower his/her activity level upon the onset of hyperactivity. These nonverbal techniques can help slow down a student and resolve the matter.

The Immoral Student

Acts of student immorality such as cheating, lying, and stealing can be devastating to the student, as well as the entire classroom. These acts of immorality are often a large temptation for students in a very competitive environment. Students who are constantly competing against other students academically, socially, or financially can easily be swayed to perform acts of immorality.

Confronting students can be a tricky situation since teachers are not always able to actually prove immoral acts. Teachers may become frustrated when their intuition suggests a student is guilty of an immoral act, but they must restrain themselves from prematurely convicting the student. However, there are several negotiating strategies that can assist the teacher in dealing with immoral students:

(*1*) Use "what if" tactic. Teachers can use the "what if" negotiating tactic. This tactic can be a very effective means of prying information out of a student in order to get the facts surrounding the immoral act itself. This information can be valuable in ascertaining the student's guilt or innocence. The teacher might state, "What if I were to tell you I have a witness who saw you commit this act." This technique is similar to what is used in a typical courtroom by a lawyer in questioning a person on the witness stand.

(*2*) Use "dumb is smart; smart is dumb" tactic. Using the "dumb is smart; smart is dumb" negotiating tactic can be an effective strategy. The teacher might confront the situation by pretending to be ignorant about any of the facts of the situation and requesting the student to help the teacher understand. While this technique may be somewhat risky in that the student may have an opportunity to create false information, the teacher may be able to contradict the student with his/her own testimony. This tactic can also be used to distract the student and allow the teacher the opportunity to assess the situation.

(*3*) Employ preventive measures. Creating an environment that is less conducive for the temptation of creating immoral acts can be very effective in reducing this problem. For example, a teacher might insure that when students are taking tests, they are well positioned away from other students. Explaining the importance of honesty and encouraging students to complete the test with confidence that they will do well can be effective.

(*4*) Confront the immorality. When catching a student in an act of immorality, the teacher should try not to humiliate the student in front of the entire class. Immoral acts are a serious matter and should be dealt with privately. Holding a conference, which includes a parent or school administrator, may be an effective option. If the student admits to an immoral act, and receives a disciplinary action, it is important to try and restore a normal relationship.

The Sleeper

Sleeping in class tends to be a bigger problem in high schools than elementary levels (Tomal, 1997b). Many students at the high school level become involved in evening activities such as work and social events and generally have less supervision and cannot be controlled as easily by their parents as elementary students. Consequently, high school students often are deprived of sufficient sleep and have a difficult time staying awake during the school day. The general "dozing off" and lack of concentration because of lack of sleep can cause significant disciplinary problems. Some ideas for negotiating with the sleeper include:

(*1*) Use nonverbals. The use of nonverbals can be an effective means of keeping a student alert. The teacher can walk close to the student and give these students more eye contact.

(*2*) Confront problem. Confronting a student about their problem may be another alternative for the teacher. The teacher may ask the student to get a drink of water or sprinkle some water on his/her face. While this is a practice a teacher may not want to reinforce on a day-to-day basis, it can be an effective means of alerting the student to the problem. The teacher should also be careful not to disregard the possibility that the sleeper may be experiencing a health problem or taking drugs that are causing him/her to be tired and sleepy in class.

(*3*) Increase activities. Involving a student in activities, such as working cooperatively with other students, completing an exercise on the board, or demonstrating, may snap the student out of the sleepy state. Many exercises that require continuous reading may reinforce student "dozing off" and altering an assignment or instructional approach can be effective.

(*4*) Counseling session. Conducting a brief counseling session with the student after class may be effective in bringing attention to the problem as well as the seriousness of it. Asking a student for the cause of the problem and requesting the student to suggest solutions can be effective in resolving the problem. Too often, students give justifiable reasons for their lack of sleep and quickly resolving the matter may not be that easy. The teacher may need to further explore the situation by involving the parents or school officials.

The Doubletalker

Students who practice "doubletalk" by giving excuses and rationalizations for their misbehavior can be irritating to any teacher. A student may respond to a teacher through a victim mentality by identifying a real or imagined problem as an excuse to compensate for his/her misbehavior or performance. Students may give excuses for not completing homework or for failing to pay attention and blame this behavior on other people or external factors. The use of excuses and doubletalk may only be a tactic for the student to get out of work or justify his/her own behavior. Some ideas in negotiating with the doubletalker include:

(*1*) Use obstinate tactics. When students give excuses (i.e., doubletalk), the teacher may use a countertactic such as using the "obstinate" tactic by not giving into the student and ignoring the student's behavior. The teacher might continue talking as if he/she did not hear the student's excuses (i.e., doubletalk). In this way, the teacher can focus on the problem and not the excuse being offered by the student.

(*2*) Conduct counseling. With the student who constantly gives excuses to justify his/her misbehavior, the teacher probably will need to counsel the student. During the counseling session, the teacher should recognize the feelings of the student, identify the root cause, agree upon a solution, and try to reinforce future positive good behavior and performance.

(*3*) Stick to rationale behavior. Recognizing that the student may be using the "doubletalk" tactic as a defense mechanism, the teacher should stick to rational adult-to-adult behavior and not become sidetracked or emotional over the student's tactic.

NEGOTIATING WITH OFFENSIVE AND VIOLENT STUDENTS

The Hostile Student

Dealing with students who become irate, angry, or hostile is a delicate situation. Students may be harboring a great deal of frustration and resentment as a result of either a dysfunctional family, social or family pressures, or personal matters. This aggression can be manifested by the student's acts of hostility in the classroom. While hostility cannot be tolerated, it is critical that the teacher deal with this problem without causing it to escalate. Techniques in negotiating with the hostile student include:

(*1*) Avoid arguing. It is generally not advisable to argue with a hostile student. Arguing with the student may only intensify the matter and create even greater hostility in the student. When frustration runs high, this hostility may cause other students to participate and the class may eventually become out of control.

(2) Discuss privately. Deal with the student privately. If the hostility occurs in the classroom, ask the student to step out in the hallway. A brief discussion in the hallway may allow the student to "save face" and rectify the problem. The teacher may then schedule a talk with the student about the situation.

(3) Use time out and quiet time. There are many variations of "time out" ranging from temporarily removing the student from participating in learning activities to removal of the student from the classroom. "Quiet time" is similar to time out, accept it usually involves directing a student to sit in a quiet area of a classroom for a few minutes and reflect upon his/her behavior. Both time out and quiet time strategies can be useful for the emotional student to contemplate his/her behavior, allow for time to cool down, and as a warning to the student.

(4) Recognize the tactic. When negotiating with the hostile student, the student's hostility may only be a tactic that is being utilized by the student in order to bargain for some position. The student may create an emotional tantrum in order to draw sympathy and produce an element of guilt in the teacher. The teacher might best deal with this tactic by ignoring the student's hostility and sticking to the facts of the matter in confronting the validity of the statements.

After resolving the facts, the teacher might then discuss with the student his/her inappropriate behavior. If a student is too emotional, the teacher might find it necessary to first concentrate on diffusing the student's behavior until the student is calm enough to discuss the disciplinary situation. Statements such as, "As soon as you become calm, we can discuss this matter," can be an effective statement to de-escalate the student's emotions.

The Harasser

The effects of harassment among students can be very damaging, not only to the student involved, but the entire school. The results of harassment can result in increased student absenteeism, anxiety and stress, sickness, decreased learning, and actual litigation. Ethically, every student should be entitled to freedom to study and participate in learning activities without any type of harassment from other students. Also, from a legal standpoint, it is "good business sense" to make efforts to prevent harassment in the school.

Harassment can take many forms from teasing other students to sexual harassment. Sexual harassment has been defined by Title VII-Section 1604.11, as any "unwelcome sexual advances, request for sexual favors, and other verbal or physical conduct of a sexual nature—when such conduct has the purpose or effect of unreasonably interfering with an individual's work performance or creating an intimidating, hostile, or offensive work environment." Some ideas for preventing harassment and handling the harasser include:

(*1*) Discuss expectations. Talk to the students and discuss the definition of harassment and effects upon people. Discuss the importance of treating people with respect and dignity, and the ramifications when people do not.

(*2*) Create positive environment. Create a positive class environment by incorporating class rules and policies against harassment. A class that has a healthy environment with low stress and tension will be less likely to advocate harassment.

(*3*) Early prevention. Do not tolerate harassers in the classroom. It is also best to confront any comments that have the potential of turning into harassing statement against others.

The Fighter

Physical fighting between students can be a difficult problem to manage depending upon the student's age. Students fighting at the elementary level tend to be more prominent than at the high school level (Tomal, 1997b). Most high school students understand the severity of physical fighting on the premises of the school and realize that this might be cause for suspension or expulsion. Recognizing this reality, students will often take their disagreements and attempt to resolve them outside the premises of the school. Fighting at the high school level generally produces more serious bodily harm than at the elementary level. Elementary students are generally more immature and allow their emotions to be displayed more easily. Given that elementary students roughly play with each other, this situation often erupts into an outright fight. Ideas for negotiating with fighters include:

(*1*) Mediation: Third party intervention may be the safest and expedient method of handling a physical fight among high school students. Calling security is generally the teacher's best option in order to maintain the safety of the teacher and fellow students.

(2) Separating students: When dealing with elementary students, immediately separate the students. Speaking sternly and forcefully, using the student's names, during this time is a key factor in gaining control. Inform the students that the matter will be dealt with and do not take sides with either of the students. Once you have separated the students, remain firm but calm. Students will recognize your behavior and be more apt to become calm themselves.

When encountering fights between high school students, a teacher should not run to the fight and intervene in an aggressive manner. The fighters may assault the teacher. The teacher should remain calm and remove any items such as necklaces and glasses from himself/herself that might potentially cause harm to the teacher. The teacher, upon arrival to the scene, should analyze the situation and look for weapons and other elements that might pose a threat to people. The teacher should yell at the fighters to stop fighting, preferably by the students' names. The teacher might separate the students by spraying water from a bottle on the students. Taking pictures can also be effective since the photos can be used for documentation, and may help the fighters stop given they usually dislike camera flashes and photos of their behavior. The teacher should also write down names of witnesses and dispense onlookers. The teacher should call appropriate school authorities (e.g., disciplinary dean, principal, and security officers), the students' parents, and police.

(3) Conducting a conference: Fighting at the high school level should always require a conference. A formal investigation (i.e., talking to witnesses and examining the fighting scene) by gaining all the facts to the altercation should precede the conference. During the conference, it is important to discuss the facts of the incident, administer appropriate disciplinary action, and attempt to set up circumstances to prevent the situation from occurring again.

The Extortioner

The extortioner uses threats of intimidation against other students to obtain items of value or patronage to which he/she is not entitled. The extortioner, who is more prevalent at the elementary level, uses coercive tactics to make his/her demands. For example, the extortioner may demand another student's lunch money, food, cap, sports cards, or school folder. Extortion takes place in and outside the school. Strategies in negotiating with extortioners include:

(*1*) Bully control: The best way to prevent extortion is to be on the alert for the bullies who commit the act. Bullies have a distinctive behavior about themselves through their aggressive and vocal mannerisms toward other students. Teachers should keep a close eye on these types of students and maintain their presence near them as much as possible especially during hall duty.

(*2*) Proactive actions: Teachers may anticipate the extortion, especially during times when students are carrying money at school for lunch and student fund-raising events by holding the money for the students. For example, the teacher might collect all the students' lunch money in the morning. Teachers can also take proactive actions by talking to students throughout the day about the problem. If a student suddenly develops a spending habit, the teacher might become a little suspicious.

Violent Offenders

Violent offenders include students who commit such acts as arson, assault, burglary, drug or gang-related incidents, homicide, robbery, sex offense, theft, trespassing, and vandalism. Schools need explicit policies and procedures in dealing with these violent offenders, such as notification of police, search protocol, incident reporting to parents and school authorities, methods of documenting offenses, and disciplinary actions. Dealing with violent offenders requires a good understanding of the legal rights of student. Some strategies in negotiating with violent offenders include:

(*1*) Surveillance cameras: The use of surveillance equipment, such as closed circuit television, can help deter crimes and protect students and school property. Cameras can be placed in critical areas of the school, such as parking lots, stairwells, bathrooms, and remote rooms.

(*2*) Restrictive measures: The use of restrictive measures such as limiting student access to facilities without special permission, parking stickers, sign-in/sign-out sheets can act as preventive techniques and anonymous information boxes. Regular hall and grounds patrol by staff can also detect and hinder potential incidents. Educating students about potential violence and defense strategies is valuable.

(*3*) Appropriate action: When a violent offense occurs, the teacher needs to take appropriate action that insures his/her safety and security of the students and school. For example, if a teacher witnesses a trespasser, he/she should never attempt to chase after the trespasser and try to apprehend him/her. The teacher places himself/herself at a high risk of being seriously harmed or killed. It is best to record as much information as possible and notify the police. Knowing when and how to take appropriate action can make the difference between a safe outcome and disaster.

When dealing with a victim of a sexual offense, call the victim's parents and police immediately, keep the victim calm, protect the crime scene, and disband onlookers. When confronted with a student with a gun, it is best not to create havoc by yelling "There's a gun!" but rather call the police and, if possible, calmly ask the student to give it up. Most violent offenses such as arson, bomb threats, robbery, burglary, assaults, and thefts should be treated like any serious crimes by calling the police and not personally taking heroic interventions.

MOTIVATING STUDENTS FOR GOOD BEHAVIOR

Motivating students, especially difficult students, is challenging for any teacher. A teacher cannot motivate anyone to learn or to behave, but the teacher can only provide circumstances in which students can motivate themselves. The old saying, "You can lead a horse to water, but you can't make them drink," is a fitting statement for the teacher in the classroom.

Understanding the drives and needs of students can help in developing circumstances to motivate students. Effective motivation requires the use of effective interpersonal communications and effective leadership skills. Every activity by students in the classroom requires some degree of motivation. Therefore, a teacher's job is to identify the drives and needs of their students and channel this behavior and help to effectively motivate them in order for them to learn and demonstrate good behavior. A fundamental basis for motivation requires the teacher to identify clear-cut goals for learning that are attainable by the students.

The accomplishment of these goals can be intrinsically enriching for the student. Given that many students have the desire for achievement, the process of learning in itself can be rewarding for students. The motivation to achieve is similar to the Japanese term called *Kaizen*. This term has been attributed to the widespread belief that the Japanese constantly drive themselves to accomplish objectives and seek improvement. This term is similar to the American drive for success and the need for taking personal responsibility for actions and outcomes. Teachers can provide motivators by establishing high, but attainable expectations for their students.

Another concept of motivation is called "social motivation." This term indicates the need for students to develop social relationships within the classroom. Students can be motivated to learn based upon the concept of social motivation by developing cooperative relationships with their peers in the learning process. The teacher must strive to set up circumstances whereby all students feel connected with their peers as well as the classroom. There are many ways to develop achievement and social motivation in students, including the following sections.

Initiate Collaborative Negotiations

It is much easier to negotiate with students from a collaborative position then from a competitive one. Collaborative negotiation is based upon the notion that both parties are willing to mutually come to an agreement. Teachers can help to establish a collaborative approach by creating positive relationships with their students.

Take a Positive View of Students

The "X" and "Y" Theory can be applied to managing discipline in the classroom and motivating students. Douglas McGregor (1960) developed a theory based upon the premise that leadership actions are a result of the leader's theory of human behavior. This idea is that the leader's assumptions about people have an implicit relationship with people's motivation. A Theory "X" leader makes assumptions that people dislike work, are inherently lazy, and need to be coerced, controlled, and threatened to obtain satisfactory behavior and performance.

A Theory "Y" leader is one who views his/her people as not being inherently lazy, but rather they are self-directed, imaginative, creative, seek responsibility and have the desire for learning. McGregor argued that is important for leaders to develop a theory "Y" mentality in order to motivate people and create a positive environment. Given that teaching is a humanistic process, developing a theory "Y" mentality is critical for the teacher in promoting positive self-concepts and a positive learning and motivating environment.

Create Self-Fulfilling Prophecies

The theory of the self-fulfilling prophecy or often called the "pygmalion effect" is also a powerful theory of human behavior. This theory suggests that a belief or expectation in an event can actually cause it to happen. Therefore, if a teacher expects positive behavior from a student, this belief can greatly influence the student to behave properly. For example, if a teacher establishes high expectations for student behavior, chances are that students will meet those expectations.

This concept can also be applied to learning. If a teacher places high expectations for learning and believes a student can achieve an outstanding grade, students will often perform to the teacher's expectations. However, this concept can act in reverse as well. If a teacher has low expectations for behavior or performance, the students may perform only at the level that meets the teacher's expectations.

Use Intrinsic Motivators

The use of intrinsic factors such as praise, personal recognition, and challenging learning activities can motivate students to behave in a classroom. Students can be intrinsically motivated by feeling a sense of personal satisfaction from completing an assignment or learning activity. Teachers can provide stimulating activities that can help promote this intrinsic motivation factor.

Use Extrinsic Motivators

Extrinsic factors such as the use of tokens, gold stars, candy, jackets, and certificates are examples of extrinsic motivators. These motivators can also help promote a positive learning environment and positive discipline in the classroom.

Talk Straight with Students

When teachers play mind games and manipulate their students through the use of doubletalk, they only reinforce a class environment that encourages misbehavior. Mind games can be any type of interaction among people that have ulterior motives instead of being honest and straightforward.

Ignore Trivial Misbehavior

It may be effective in certain instances for the teacher to ignore trivial misbehavior. A teacher must use good judgment when deciding when to "nip the problem in the bud," or to ignore the behavior. Sometimes students may use trivial misbehavior in order to gain attention from the teacher. If the teacher ignores this misbehavior, the student may stop misbehaving or prevent the incident from escalating.

Allow Students to "Save Face"

The teacher should always try and let the student to "save face." Students generally have a very high degree of peer identification and any embarrassment in front of a student's peers can be devastating for his/her self-esteem. Not only is it potentially damaging for a teacher to discipline a student in front of his/her peers, but it can also have a negative impact on the class as a whole. When students see a student being disciplined in front of the class, they may all feel as if they are being reprimanded.

Keep Communication Open

Keeping the lines of communication open between the teacher and student is important to maintaining healthy personal relationships. Students need to feel that they are respected by the teacher and are able to talk with the teacher without fear and humiliation. It is not uncommon for a teacher to attempt to stifle a misbehaving student by criticizing the student very harshly. While the misbehavior may stop, the student may harbor ill feelings and resentment towards the teacher. The teacher may not recognize these "pent-up" feelings, which may negatively effect the student's learning.

Challenge Distorted Thinking

A teacher should not allow students to make distorted and inaccurate comments such as false information about students, school policies, or classroom rules. This situation can create rumors and cause other students to misbehave.

Recognize Defense Mechanisms

Teachers should also recognize the multitude of defense mechanisms used by students. Students will often use defense mechanisms, such as denial, projection, fantasy/idealization, or reaction formation. While these may be difficult situations, the teacher needs to counsel his/her students or obtain professional help for the student.

Use Positive Self-Talk

A technique of using positive "self-talk" can be a valuable strategy in helping students recognize and take ownership and responsibility for their own misbehavior. "Self-talk" is a technique whereby people silently talk to themselves and rationalize situations in their mind. Self-talk can be either positive or negative. When used in a negative manner, people embellish situations or create "mountains out of molehills." Positive self-talk can be valuable when a person logically looks at a situation in an objective manner and makes the appropriate changes.

IMPROVING YOUR NEGOTIATING POSITION

Every teacher will eventually face the challenging student. Examples of challenging students are chronic talkers, know-it-alls, harassers, violent offenders, and students who are hostile, defiant, and insubordinate. The underlying reason for the student's behavior may be varied. The student may be experiencing girlfriend or boyfriend problems, pressure at home, health concerns, threats from gangs, learning difficulties, or psychological problems. The student may also be harboring resentment against the teacher, feel incompetent, or lack confidence in their academic abilities. In negotiating with challenging students, it is important for the teacher to identify the underlying issue for their misbehavior. Some general guidelines and principles in negotiating with challenging students include:

Confront Feelings

If the student is experiencing strong emotions of anger and frustration, his/her behavior may be manifested through open defiance. In these cases, teachers need to communicate with the student. The teacher might start by asking the student how he/she is feeling about the behavior. In this way, the teacher might be able to personalize the relationship and draw out the student's reason for the behavior. Students often base their behavior upon the emotions they are feeling at any given time. The goal of the teacher is to reduce the student's strong emotions in order to help the student approach the problem from a more logical basis. By confronting the student's feelings, the student is more likely to believe that the teacher cares about him/her as an individual. Dealing with the student's emotions and feelings can also be the first step in de-escalating a conflict situation and begin negotiations.

Concession Making

Concession making means giving up (conceding) something in order to open up negotiations. For example, when dealing with a child with low self-esteem, the teacher might begin by praising the student for past good behavior or performance. Praising the student during times of conflict is actually making a concession. Rather than confronting the student and escalating the situation, it may be more effective to open up discussions through giving concessions.

If the student is praised for his/her work, the student may appreciate this recognition and accommodate the teacher's request by talking with the teacher about his/her behavioral problems. For example, if a student is not feeling confident with his/her performance, building the student's self-esteem can be the first step in motivating the student to improve. Students with low self-esteem need constant praise and personal attention.

Modify Expectations

Modifying the expectations for a student may be an effective technique for students who are experiencing academic difficulties. If the challenging student is refusing to work, the teacher might bargain with the student by suggesting that the student complete the work in segments or through an alternate method. For example, the teacher might ask the student for suggestions in how the student might complete the assignment, or the teacher might suggest first completing a portion of the assignment. This method of reducing expectations on how work is competed allows the student to save face, become more responsible for the work, and to take an active role in working with the teacher.

There is always room for negotiation when it comes to helping students learn. Every student has different needs; and if the teacher is willing to be flexible, students will ultimately become more responsible themselves. A teacher who is viewed as being too rigid and controlling may stifle the student's motivation.

Patience

Teachers can improve their negotiating success with students by developing the virtue of patience. Developing patience can be very effective for knowing when to avoid confronting a disciplinary situation. For example, when a student misbehaves, the teacher might ask the student to step out in the hall or to the back of the room for a few moments as an excuse to give this time for the student to contemplate his/her behavior.

The teacher needs to be careful not to embarrass or humiliate the student. While every situation calls for a judgement call on behalf of the teacher, selecting the most appropriate disciplinary approach can be the key to resolving the misbehavior.

Confront the Misbehavior

When faced with a challenging student, it may be best to confront the misbehavior through a formal disciplinary session. During this session, the teacher can address the magnitude of the behavior and explore underlying issues, and actions for eliminating the misbehavior. The formal session adds a serious dimension to the problem versus simply addressing the misbehavior in the classroom.

CHAPTER 8

Implementing Discipline by Negotiation

DEVELOPING A UNIFORM DISCIPLINE POLICY

ONE OF THE most important factors in helping to insure good student behavior in the school and classroom is the establishment of a uniform school disciplinary policy. Every district should have a policy that specifies the district's rules, guidelines for student behavior, student responsibilities, rights of parents, teacher, and students, and procedures of disciplinary action for student misconduct.

Once a uniform school disciplinary policy is established, all teachers and staff need to be well-trained in understanding the policy to insure that it is consistently administered. The policy should be well-documented and distributed to all students, parents, and staff members. The school discipline policy should be consistent with state school codes and labor agreements among district employee groups (e.g., unions). Every school policy should also contain guidelines for students with disabilities and state and federal laws concerning rights of individuals. A fundamental right of all students is a safe school environment.

The school uniform discipline policy should include the guidelines for student, parent, teacher, and staff rights and responsibilities (see the School Uniform Discipline Policy for the Chicago Public Schools in Appendix A). Students should understand rules and expectations regarding attendance, standards of dress and grooming, citizenship, academic achievement, and extracurricular activities. Once students have a clear understanding of their responsibilities and codes of conduct, then the job of enforcing and administering discipline is easier.

The rights of students have evolved since the early 1800s when schools emphasized self-control and punishable offenses, which even included leg shackles as routine methods of controlling misbehavior. In fact, Horace Mann, the father of American education, characterized the discipline of students based upon the use of authority, fear, pain, and

113

punishment. Humiliation in front of other students was commonplace. For students who misbehaved, primitive forms of control were often used in the classroom to control behavior.

As methods of controlling misbehavior evolved, the use of corporal punishment was widespread. The American education system has used an authoritarian approach as a basis for school discipline. As late as 1988, Gallup and Elam (1988) reported that corporal punishment was still being widely used and viewed favorably by educators and the public.

More recent policies in school discipline tend to support a more humanistic approach based upon mutual respect and trust among students and teachers. With the passage of federal laws, the need to treat students as individuals with common rights has brought forth a more humanitarian approach to school discipline. Typical areas of student rights include the open access to public school education, the rights to appeal decisions regarding absence and grades, due process in disciplinary matters, and the availability of counseling and special services for substance abuse, health, and disability problems.

Teachers should avoid using disciplinary approaches that may belittle a student in front of their peers, such as putting the student's name on the blackboard as a display of misbehavior to the entire class. While there may be temptation to utilize these methods, given that they can be effective in producing short-term results, they can be damaging for a student's self-esteem. Discipline should be a private matter and publicly displaying a student's name in front of his/her peers, with associated points for misbehavior, might intensify emotional reactions, especially in emotionally disturbed students. School policies, like class rules, should be written in a positive manner versus a negative one. For example, a rule might state that "Students should always walk in the hallways," instead of "There will be no running in the hallways."

A school disciplinary policy should include the rights and responsibilities of parents, teachers, and staff. Some typical parent responsibilities include access to student records, encouragement of participation in the student's education, encouragement of involvement in the school process, and the right to appeal for disciplinary and academic matters. A school policy should clearly delineate the responsibilities of teachers and allow them to be consistent, fair, and firm in dealing with student misconduct.

The school uniform policy should contain provisions that insure the safety and security of students, staff, and teachers. The responsibilities and rights of administrators and staff should also be provided, which include such areas as conducting school matters with professional ethics, keeping parents and the community informed on educational matters, and having a genuine concern for working with the parents and community for the education of students.

REASONS FOR DISCIPLINING STUDENTS

There are several reasons for disciplining students for misbehavior such as deterrence, correction, punishment, and legal reasons (see Figure 8.1). Educators should consider the reason why a student is being disciplined before administering disciplinary action. This can help insure that the most effective action is being given to the student, and that the action is in line with the best interests of the school.

The use of deterrence is used by an educator to prevent other students from following the same actions of the misbehaving student. Deterrence can be very helpful for serious matters in which educators feel that it is necessary to prevent other students from engaging in this type of action. For example, for high-profile acts of violence that have the potential for continued disruption of the school, such as gang activity, battery, theft, destruction of school property, drug and contraband use, disciplining a student based upon deterrence can be good justification. The expulsion of the violent student may be necessary to deter others from this same behavior.

Corrective Action

The objective of corrective action is to alter or reform the student's behavior to acceptable behavior. Corrective action may be the main reason

Discipline Reasons	Rationale
1. Deterrence	1. Make example to others
2. Correction	2. Change behavior
3. Punishment	3. Show seriousness of act
4. School order	4. Safety of students
5. Legal	5. Abide by laws/policies

Figure 8.1. Reasons for disciplining students.

for administering discipline to a student who commits a low-profile act such as continued absenteeism, emotional tantrums, or disrespect to the teacher. The student's act may be one that has little impact on the overall school and may be symptomatic of underlying emotional problems within the student.

Punishment

The use of punishment may be the main reason for taking disciplinary action against a student. While punishment should not be the prime reason for disciplining a child, it may be necessary in rare or extreme cases as a "wake-up call" for the student in understanding the severe gravity of an act. For example, spanking a child by a parent is not generally appropriate or effective, however, in rare situations where the child's actions may put his/her own and others' life at risk, a parent may be warranted in spanking the child if done out of love and respect. In the school system, other means, rather than corporal punishment, should be used for punishment, such as suspension or detention.

Legal

Legal factors may dictate the reason for disciplining a student. The need to obey federal and state laws requires educators to take disciplinary action against a student for committing specific illegal activities. Activities such as aggravated assault, arson, bomb threats, burglary, theft, and other violent acts require the school to take action against students.

While all four reasons, to some extent, may be included when taking disciplinary action against a student, selecting the primary reason can help achieve efficacy. As a general matter, discipline should be administered to students with the following guidelines and conditions for positive discipline:

(1) Students should have the right to know what is expected of them regarding their academic performance and behavior.
(2) Schools should utilize a preventive disciplinary approach based upon progressive discipline.
(3) Schools should employ a "hot stove" approach which consists of disciplinary action being: immediate, consistent, and impersonal.

(*4*) Disciplinary action should always be administered, when possible, in a private setting.

(*5*) Humiliation and intimidation of students should be avoided.

(*6*) Teachers and staff should strive to provide positive support for students.

(*7*) Students should have the right for open and honest communication during the discipline process.

(*8*) Teachers should respect the feelings and legal rights of the student as a human being.

(*9*) Discipline policies should be written based upon the needs and rules of the school.

(*10*) Allegations of student misconduct should always be thoroughly investigated to insure fairness for the student.

(*11*) Discipline should be administered to students with firmness and fairness.

(*12*) Discipline should be administered based upon negotiation that considers each student's mitigating and extenuating circumstances.

(*13*) Once discipline has been administered, the teacher should attempt to resume a normal relationship with the student.

DEVELOPING A PROGRESSIVE DISCIPLINE PROGRAM

The process of taking disciplinary action should be one that is instructional and corrective, not punitive. The model of progressive discipline is the best means for dealing with students with due process, fairness, and one in which extenuating circumstances can be considered.

The goal of progressive discipline is to give the student an opportunity for self-correction prior to taking more serious measures. Progressive discipline attempts to improve students' behavior for the future rather than punish the student by focusing on the past. Acts of student misconduct are ranked from least severe to most severe in the progressive discipline approach as follows:

(*1*) Counseling

(*2*) Verbal warning (including teacher–student and/or parent conference or detention/in school before or after)

(*3*) Written warning (including disciplinary dean conference)

(*4*) Suspension (including varying degrees of days suspended)

(*5*) Suspension and disciplinary reassignment

(*6*) Expulsion

Stage 1: Counseling

The first stage of discipline, which is considered a pre-step level, is counseling the student. Counseling can be considered as talking with a student for any academic or behavior that is undesirable, but is short of requiring disciplinary action. Counseling is concerned with upgrading the student's academic performance or behavior from a non-disciplinary approach.

Student behaviors that may warrant counseling with a student include general talking without permission, horseplay, low motivation or apathy, tardiness, and any other type of disruptive behavior that hinders the orderly process of classroom teaching. At this level, the teacher makes a judgment call as to whether to talk with the student or to impose some type of disciplinary action. Generally speaking, the counseling stage can be viewed as a warning step for the student in an attempt to rectify any academic or behavioral problem before it becomes a problem.

There are a variety of methods of talking with the student during the counseling stage. The teacher may choose to have a short discussion with the student about his/her behavior, or a more formal discussion by actually asking the student to stay after school. The teacher, during the counseling session, should take time to get the facts from the student, describe the behavioral or performance desired expectations, actively listen to the student, obtain agreement for resolving the problem, and provide positive reinforcement for future performance. The teacher should also inform the student of disciplinary consequences for continued inappropriate behavior or performance.

During this counseling level, the teacher's objective is to eliminate the problem during the early stages and prevent the misbehavior from escalating. Essentially, the teacher conducts a discussion with the student in an attempt to reach a quick and amicable settlement. The interchange may be brief, consisting of a few statements whereby the student might conclude the interaction by stating "I get the message, sorry. I'll do better." Conducting a brief counseling session at the early stages of a discipline problem can be more valuable than a lengthy formal one. For example, taking disciplinary action against a student may be viewed as "overkill" by the student and may only cause more harm. Students often have a good view of a sense of fairness and can harbor feelings of resentment if they feel an action is excessive.

Another effective technique that can be used during the counseling stage, especially at the elementary level is called "quiet time." After counseling a student, the teacher may opt to remove the student from the activity and provide a few minutes for a child and ask the student to sit quietly alone and contemplate his/her behavior. Giving the student these moments of quiet time can allow him/her to reflect upon his/her behavior, recognize the magnitude of the problem, and make a better transition back to learning activities. Given that other students may witness the quiet time, the teacher should be careful not to make a spectacle out of the student and belittle the student in front of his/her peers.

After the student has remained quiet for a prescribed amount of time, the teacher can ask the student to continue working on the prior activity. Once the student returns to work, the teacher should attempt to find examples of praise for the student in order to restore a healthy relationship. Teachers should also be careful that the use of quiet time doesn't backfire by allowing the student to gain peer recognition by becoming the center of attention. For younger children, requesting the student to rest his/her head on the desk for a few moments may also be a quick and effective variation.

The use of quiet time can be also used for the entire class. If a teacher has an entire class that is disruptive, the teacher could counsel this class, as with an individual student. The teacher may find it necessary to gain the attention of a disruptive class by counseling them regarding their inappropriate behavior and requesting that all students stop what they are doing for a few minutes of quiet time. The sooner the teacher can effectively obtain silence within the classroom, the greater the chances of success. Once the class has effectively remained silent for a few minutes, the teacher should attempt to restore normal learning activities and praise them for their good performance.

The counseling session can also be used to give constructive feedback to the student. The teacher can focus both on the student's positive behavior as well as the misbehavior. Some constructive characteristics in giving student feedback include the following:

(*1*) Be specific. The teacher should be specific and to the point about the student's inadequate performance or misbehavior. If the student is not turning in homework assignments, the teacher should cite specific days and actual assignments, rather than talk in general. Should the problem be a behavioral problem such as talking without permission, the teacher should indicate the specific misbehavior and give examples. The teacher should also indicate the desired behavior and agreed upon rules of the classroom.

(2) Focus on student behavior, not on personality. The teacher should describe behavioral aspects of the student versus discussing aspects of the student's personality. For example, if a student is constantly dominating discussion in the classroom, the teacher should state that, "You are talking much more than the other students," as opposed to stating, "You are a showboat and a loudmouth." By focusing on behaviors, the student is better able to adjust his/her behavior versus feeling that the behavior is due to a fixed personality trait that may be perceived by the student as being more difficult to change. Moreover, by focusing on behavior, the teacher does not attack the student's self-esteem and the student is more apt to save face.

(3) Focus on one problem at a time. When giving feedback to a student, a teacher should not overwhelm the student with several problems; rather, focus on one, or at most two, behavioral problems. The student is better able to work correcting one or two problems versus several problems at a time. For example, if a student has been demonstrating several inappropriate behaviors, such as apathy, talking out of turn, general defiance, and lack of respect to the teacher and classmates, the teacher may want to first focus on the more serious concern and work on the others at a later time.

(4) Identify the root cause of the problem. Identifying the root cause of a behavior problem is one of the first steps in resolving a disciplinary matter. Attempting to solve the problem based upon a proposed solution without identifying the problem is an invitation for disaster. For example, if a student is displaying apathy, the teacher might try to identify the cause of the problem instead of commanding the student to become more motivated.

(5) Feedback should be immediate. When giving feedback, talk to the student immediately following a behavioral incident rather than waiting too long. While it may be difficult to discuss a behavioral problem with a student in the middle of class, the teacher should attempt to talk with the student as soon as time permits. However, in some cases it may be desirable to wait to talk with a student, such as when a student is in a highly emotional state, to allow time for the student to calm down. Giving immediate feedback to a student allows the student to recognize his/her behavior and take responsibility for changing it.

(6) Direct feedback that is within control of the student. Far too often, teachers criticize students for behavior that they have no control over such as the rowdiness of fellow classmates. No student likes to

be disciplined for the misbehavior of a group of students because of his/her association with the group. Teachers should avoid general comments such as, "This entire class needs to shape up" when in fact, many of the students have no control over the students around them. By focusing on the general problem, the student may feel that the criticism is unfair and prejudiced.

(7) Utilize a collaborative process. Giving constructive feedback to a student involves two-way communication. The need to hold a collaborative discussion allows the student to develop ownership in resolving the problem. Collaborative discussions foster a more open environment in developing mutual respect.

(8) Provide positive reinforcement. It is important that the teacher maintain a positive outlook and give positive reinforcement when counseling a student. The mere inflection of a voice or negative body language can send signals of belittling the student. The student needs to believe that the teacher is sincerely concerned for the student and is willing to collaborate and work together in helping the student improve.

(9) Develop a contract with the student. When giving feedback to a student, it may be necessary to actually develop a verbal agreement or written contract with the student as to the expected behavior. If the teacher is counseling with the student, the teacher might elect to write a statement outlining the misconduct and the agreed upon plan of corrective action.

(10) Summarize agreements. When conducting a counseling session with a student, the teacher should always conclude the session by summarizing what has been said, the agreement for corrective action, future follow-up, and a personal statement of endorsement indicating belief in the student for change. While the session should always be end on a positive note, the teacher may want to inform the student of additional consequences if the behavior is not improved.

Stage 2: Verbal Warning

Stage two of the progressive discipline approach is called the verbal warning. The purpose of the verbal warning stage is to give the student a verbal reprimand for his/her misbehavior or poor performance. The verbal warning is considered the first stage of the progressive discipline level. The verbal warning stage should be conducted for various lower level acts of student misconduct, such as cheating, leaving the classroom without permission, improper dress, loitering, persistent tardiness, and failing to attend class with a valid excuse.

Depending upon the student's grade level, a number of disciplinary actions can be taken against the student such as in-house detention, loss of recess, teacher-student conference, parent conference, or conference with the disciplinary dean. During this session, the teacher should discuss any previous counseling sessions, identify the root cause of the problem for misbehavior, outline an action for improvement, and state the consequences for continued misbehavior.

During the verbal warning stage, the teacher should document the session by writing a summary report and putting it in the student's file. The teacher might also allow the student to keep a copy of the report.

Stage 3: Written Warning

Stage three is called the written warning. The purpose of the written warning is to document with a letter the student's specific behavioral performance problem and disciplinary action given. This letter should be signed by the student and a copy sent to the student's parents. The written warning stage serves to send a strong signal to the student that his/her behavior or performance is unacceptable. Student offenses that might warrant a written reprimand include fighting, use of profanity, serious disobedience, forgery, serious disruptive behavior on a school bus or in a classroom, gambling, and various acts of immorality and harassment.

There are several disciplinary actions depending upon mitigating circumstances that can be taken at this stage, which include a teacher-parent conference, in-school suspension, detention, and possible suspension from school (e.g., one to five days).

During the written warning conference, the teacher should review all past communication, past disciplinary actions, resolve the root cause of the problem, develop an action plan, state consequences for continued misbehavior, resolve the matter, and establish a normal relationship as soon as possible. Variations of the written warning stage may include giving the student a prescribed number of days to improve upon, place the student on a probationary behavior period, or possible disciplinary reassignment.

One feature of the written warning is that it allows for an opportunity to clearly document the student's poor behavior or performance by a letter, which should be sent to the student, parents, and file. This letter should be signed by the student. After the written warning conference, a teacher should also follow-up with the student and conduct a meeting on the student's progress.

Stage 4: Suspension

The fourth stage of progressive discipline is called suspension. Suspension should be reserved for very serious student misconduct or chronic misbehavior. Serious disruption of the educational process is not limited to the classroom, but might include acts committed while on the school grounds that directly affect the operation of the school, such as activating a false fire alarm, assault, vandalism, fighting, theft, extortion, or possession of prohibited electronic devices and fireworks.

Various disciplinary actions that can be taken against the student in this stage include in-school suspension, detention, parent-administrator conference, disciplinary reassignment, and police notification. During the suspension conference, the teacher must insure that the rights of the student are not violated, due process is undertaken, the facts of the situation are carefully analyzed, and the student understands the very serious nature of the behavior and consequences of possible expulsion.

Stage 5: Expulsion

The last stage of the progressive discipline is called expulsion. When a student's misconduct is illegal or seriously disrupts the orderly learning environment, expulsion is the last resort. The school has no choice but to exclude a student with anti-social or incorrigible behavior. Arson, bomb threats, possession or use of weapons, robbery, burglary, sex violations, gang activity, gross disobedience, and possession or concealment of a firearm or destructive device are examples of these serious acts of misconduct.

Expulsion involves the removal of a student from school for a period of time often ranging between two weeks to two years. Given the serious nature of expulsion, this stage requires a formal due process hearing including written notification of the charges. The disciplinary action conducted at the hearing may also include disciplinary reassignment, police notification, and arresting of the student by police.

The administering of expulsion sends a message to the student that his/her behavior is incompatible with the goals and safe operation of the school. The student must be afforded procedural due process. The student should be able to defend himself/herself against all accusations and an orderly process and hearing should be mandatory. The student should also be given a written notice of the charges against him/her and should be entitled to discovery of facts and allowed to seek legal counsel. Prior to the hearing, the student should be made aware of the rules and regulations which have been violated.

During the hearing, mitigating circumstances can be included in negotiating a disciplinary action. The student, with representation, should be allowed to present his/her case and be allowed appeals. The mitigating circumstances might include the background of the student, the nature of the incident itself or chronic behavior, specifics in the alleged charges against the student, and the facts surrounding the situation. The student should also be informed of his/her procedural rights and any defense process available to him/her. Procedural rights might include appeal systems, the time factors, right to confront accusers, and right to produce and cross-examine witnesses and produce affidavits.

The student should be given adequate time to prepare for his/her defense. Unless there are extenuating circumstances, generally five to ten days is appropriate. The student may attempt to negotiate longer periods of preparation time. During the hearing, the school should attempt to have the case heard by an impartial bearer. The student should also be given ample opportunity for negotiation at the hearing prior to being expelled.

The goal of the hearing should be to arrive at an acceptable outcome even if it includes expulsion. When the disciplinary action involves special education students, special due process procedures relative to state and federal laws need to be considered. Also, while the expulsion stage can be considered a final stage of progressive disciplinary action, the school should conclude the session by making attempts to restore a normal relationship with the student. In all likelihood, the student will eventually return to school and it is important that his/her learning process continues.

ESTABLISHING A PEER MEDIATION PROGRAM

An effective process in helping resolve student disciplinary problems is called peer mediation. This negotiation-based process assists students in resolving conflict through mediation from their peers. Rather than a teacher resolving the conflict among students, the students can work with a trained peer in mediating their differences. The premise of peer mediation is to allow students to negotiate and work out their differences themselves rather than through a higher authority. When students are able to work out their differences among themselves, they may be more apt to accept responsibility for their behavior, resolve the conflict, and be more motivated for good behavior in the classroom.

The process of peer mediation begins with conducting a series of awareness sessions for all the teachers and staff in how the process is utilized. Once this training has occurred, a pool of student peer mediators is selected. This pool of peer mediators is then trained in mediation, negotiation strategies, communication, effective listening, and conflict resolution. Once the peer mediators have been trained and all necessary forms have been developed, the process begins.

When a teacher experiences a conflict situation between two students, the teacher can fill out a form and request that the students mediate their differences through the peer mediation process. The students then would meet with the peer mediator at a predetermined time that does not disrupt normal school schedule and activities to resolve their differences. In this mediation session, the students working with the peer mediator negotiate their differences. The students would examine the situation, discuss the feelings involved in the conflict and how their feelings differ from each other.

Another feature of this process is that the students often utilize worksheets in describing the situation, the feelings involved, and reaching agreement for resolution. Besides resolving the conflict, another benefit of peer mediation is that the students actually learn how to effectively handle conflict in life and develop interpersonal relations skills.

The peer mediation process should be tailored by the school to fit their needs. For example, video tapes on conflict resolution, behavioral assessment instruments, conflict resolution surveys, and mediation strategies and techniques can be utilized. A typical strategy is to ask the students who are having a conflict whether they should do the following:

(*1*) Yell at the person.
(*2*) Call the person names.
(*3*) Explain how you feel.
(*4*) Try to understand how the other student feels.
(*5*) Refuse to talk with the other student.
(*6*) Ask for help in resolving the conflict.
(*7*) Try to listen to the other person.

(*8*) Control your feelings and emotions.
(*9*) Try to be open and objective in understanding the conflict.

Another technique used to help students resolve conflict during the session is to ask the students to draw a picture that illustrates the conflict and use of the words that are being said. Depending upon the student's grade level, younger students may also draw a picture of the faces of the students in conflict, illustrating how they feel. Other instruments and worksheets might consist of assessing the student's feelings toward conflict or questions that ask for ideas in resolving the conflict situation. Questions might consist of "What ideas do you have for resolving the matter?" "When conflict arises, what should people do?" "What are the negative results of unresolved conflict?" and "What are positive outcomes for effectively resolving conflict situations?"

IMPLEMENTING THE DISCIPLINE BY NEGOTIATION PROGRAM

The Discipline by Negotiation Program can be implemented in either a school or an entire district. Restoring sanity and safety to our schools through Discipline by Negotiation is the responsibility of everyone in the school and community. The steps in implementing the program are described below:

(*1*) Establish school vision.
(*2*) Conduct awareness sessions.
(*3*) Conduct organizational assessment.
(*4*) Conduct benchmarking of discipline program.
(*5*) Review and revise the school discipline policy.
(*6*) Establish or revise progressive discipline procedure.
(*7*) Develop a Peer Mediation program.
(*8*) Train teachers and staff.
(*9*) Implement Discipline by Negotiation program.
(*10*) Evaluate results and continuously improve program.

Step 1: Establish Vision

The first step in implementing the program is to establish a committee representing various stakeholders in the community (e.g., parents, teachers, administrators, community members, students). This committee should create a vision plan that includes a vision statement, goals, and procedures in reducing disciplinary problems. The vision plan serves as a foundation for the ongoing process and helps to maintain a concise picture of the desired outcomes of the program. The committee can also help to motivate people, overcome roadblocks, and provide resources for the program.

Step 2: Conduct Awareness Sessions

Once the vision plan is established, a series of awareness sessions should be conducted for all teachers, staff, and interested community members explaining the vision plan. The committee might also send a letter to all parents explaining the vision plan. Communication is critical at this stage to ensure that everyone understands the program and responsibilities.

Step 3: Conduct Organizational Assessment

An organizational assessment of the school should be conducted in step three to identify the organization's strengths and areas in need of improvement that impact upon the behavior of students. For example, a survey might be conducted assessing the opinions of respondents about school safety and security, discipline policies, administration of discipline policies, leadership, student-centered programs, facilities and resources, scheduling of staff and classes, and curriculum and instruction. This assessment is important so that the areas in need of improvement that impact discipline can be identified.

Step 4: Conduct Benchmarking of Discipline Program

Step four consists of the benchmarking, which means identifying the best discipline practices of other schools as a basis for tailoring the Discipline by Negotiation program. For example, a benchmarking team might be established to conduct the process by contacting and obtaining other school discipline policies, progressive discipline plans, peer mediation programs, safety and security procedures, and other programs related to discipline.

Step 5: Review and Revise Discipline Policy

After reviewing the benchmarking information, the organization's discipline policy should then be reviewed and revised. A policy team, working with the disciplinary dean(s), could be established to develop the policy.

Step 6: Establish or Revise Progressive Discipline Program

Step six consists of developing a progressive discipline program that is best for the organization. This program should be clearly stated and approved by the steering committee and school board.

Step 7: Develop Peer Mediation Program

The development of a peer mediation program is step seven. This program should be developed based upon the school discipline policy and progressive discipline program. The program should be piloted using volunteer students and teachers.

Step 8: Train Teachers and Staff

Step eight consists of training teachers and staff in the Discipline by Negotiation program. This program includes the school policy, administration of the policy, progressive discipline procedure, peer mediation program, and training in the principles and techniques of Discipline by Negotiation. For example, the program could be conducted for teachers and staff as part of their inservice development. Miniature follow-up sessions could also be conducted to reinforce the principles and skills learned.

Step 9: Implement the Program

Once the teachers and staff have been trained, step nine consists of actually implementing the Discipline by Negotiation program. The students should be informed of the program including the new policies and procedures. Also, all new disciplinary forms and information should be distributed.

Step 10: Evaluation and Continuous Improvement

After the program has been implemented, it should be periodically evaluated by measuring such areas as teacher, staff, and students' opinions about the program, rate of disciplinary offenses, corrective actions taken, and related discipline information.

SUMMARY

Restoring sanity and safety to schools is an art that relies upon a great deal of interpersonal communication, awareness of human needs, and a keen sense of negotiating "street smarts." Negotiation should not be viewed as a panacea for eliminating disciplinary problems, but it can offer a viable alternative approach for a school or district.

School Uniform Code: Chicago Public Schools

STUDENT MISCONDUCT

THIS SECTION DESCRIBES a broad range of misconduct that is prohibited in school. Because the following sections listing acts of misconduct do not include all types of misconduct, the student who commits an act of misconduct not listed under the sections herein shall be subjected to the discretionary authority of the classroom teacher and the principal or designee.

All disciplinary actions for misconduct should include a conference between the teacher and/or principal or designee and the student, followed by notification to the parent(s) or guardian. The student, parent, or guardian who feels that the disciplinary action taken is unwarranted has the right to appeal to the principal. The next level of appeal is the region education officer. The disciplinary process is intended to be instructional and corrective, not punitive.

The policies and administrative procedures apply to actions of students during school hours, before and after school, while on school property, while traveling on vehicles funded by the Board of Trustees, at all school-sponsored events, and when the actions affect the mission or operation of the Chicago Public Schools. Students may also be subject to discipline for serious acts of misconduct which occur either off-campus or during non-school hours when the misconduct disrupts the orderly educational process in the Chicago Public Schools.

The Uniform Discipline Code shall be followed and enforced in the same spirit and manner throughout the school system. The range of actions is listed from the least severe to the most severe. Staff members shall consider all mitigating circumstances prior to disciplinary action and ensure due process for each student. Mitigating circumstances include, but are not limited to, the following factors:

- age, health, maturity, and academic placement of a student
- prior conduct
- attitude of a student

- cooperation of parents
- willingness to make restitution
- seriousness of offense
- willingness to enroll in a student assistance program

Group 1—Acts of Misconduct

These acts of misconduct include *inappropriate* student behaviors in the classroom or on the school grounds, such as the following:

1-1 Running and/or making excessive noise in the hall or building
1-2 Cheating and/or copying the work of another student
1-3 Leaving the classroom without permission
1-4 Being improperly dressed
1-5 Initiating or participating in any unacceptable physical contact
1-6 Displaying any behavior that is disruptive to the orderly process of classroom instruction
1-7 Loitering
1-8 Failing to attend class without a valid excuse
1-9 Persistent tardiness to school or class

Disciplinary Action—First Violation

Minimum	*Maximum*
Teacher–Student Conference	Teacher–Student–Parent Conference

Repeated or Flagrant Violation

Minimum	*Maximum*
Teacher–Student–Parent– Resource Person–Administrator Conference	In-School Suspension

Group 2—Acts of Misconduct

These acts of misconduct include those student behaviors that *disrupt* the orderly educational process in the school or on the school grounds, such as the following:

2-1 Posting or distributing unauthorized or other written materials on school grounds
2-2 Leaving the school without permission
2-3 Interfering with school authorities and programs through walkouts or sit-ins

2-4 Exhibiting any hostile physical actions
2-5 Failing to abide by school rules and regulations
2-6 Using or publishing profane, obscene, indecent, immoral, libelous, or offensive language and/or gestures
2-7 Use or possession of tobacco products
2-8 Defying (disobeying) the authority of school personnel
2-9 Failing to provide proper identification Unauthorized use of school parking or other areas

Disciplinary Action—First Violation

Minimum	*Maximum*
Teacher–Student Conference	Teacher–Student–Parent–Resource Person–Administrator Conference

Repeated or Flagrant Violation

Minimum	*Maximum*
In-School Suspension	Suspension (1–5 days) or Disciplinary Reassignment

Group 3—Acts of Misconduct

These acts of misconduct include those student behaviors that *seriously* disrupt the orderly educational process in the classroom, in the school, and/or on the school grounds, such as the following:

3-1 Disruptive behavior on the school bus
3-2 Gambling
3-3 Fighting—two people, no injuries
3-4 Profane, obscene, indecent, immoral, or seriously offensive language and gestures, propositions, exhibitings, or sexual harassment
3-5 Persisting in serious acts of disobedience or misconduct
3-6 Any behavior that is seriously disruptive
3-7 Forgery

Disciplinary Action—First Violation

Minimum	*Maximum*
Teacher–Student–Parent–Resource Person–Administrator Conference	Suspension (1–5 days)

Repeated or Flagrant Violation

Minimum	*Maximum*
Suspension (1–5 days)	Suspension (6–10 days) Disciplinary Reassignment and/or Reassignment

Group 4—Acts of Misconduct

These acts of misconduct include those student behaviors that *very seriously* disrupt the orderly educational process in the classroom, in the school, and/or on the school grounds. In most cases, these behaviors are also illegal, such as the following:

4-1 False activation of a fire alarm
4-2 Extortion
4-3 Assault
4-4 Vandalism or criminal damage to property
4-5 Battery
4-6 Fighting—more than two people and involves injury or injuries
4-7 Theft or possession of property not exceeding $150 in value
4-8 Possession, use, or delivery of fireworks
4-9 Possession, use, or delivery of pagers, cellular telephones, and/or other prohibited electronic devices

Disciplinary Action

Minimum	*Maximum*
Teacher–Student–Parent–Resource Person–Administrator Conference	Suspension (1–10 days), Disciplinary Reassignment, and Police Notification

Note: If it is determined that the student's misconduct is related to the student's disability and disciplinary measures must be taken, contact Implementation Monitoring. Students with disabilities, even if expelled, must be provided education in an alternative education setting.

National Association of Secondary School Principals Violence in the Media and Entertainment Industry Position Statement

WHEREAS   IN 1979, the National Association of Secondary School Principals urged the broadcasting and motion picture industries to work with educators and parents in moving toward a significant reduction of violent acts in television and film programming;

Whereas   the nation is experiencing an unrivaled period of juvenile violent crime perpetrated by youths from all races, social classes, and lifestyles;

Whereas   the average American child views 8,000 murders and 100,000 acts of violence on TV before finishing elementary school, and by the age of 18, that same teenager will have witnessed 200,000 acts of violence on TV, including 40,000 murders; and,

Whereas   the entertainment industry (movies, records, music videos, radio, and television) plays an important role in fostering antisocial behavior by promoting instant gratification, glorifying casual sex, encouraging the use of profanity, nudity, violence, killing, and racial and sexual stereotyping; be it therefore known that, The National Association of Secondary School Principals:

- appreciates the efforts of the U.S. Attorney General to focus on the problem of increasing violence in the media;
- stands in opposition to violence and insensitive behavior and dialogue in the entertainment industry;
- commends television broadcasters who have begun self-regulation by labeling each program it deems potentially offensive with the following warning: DUE TO VIOLENT CONTENT, PARENTAL DISCRETION IS ADVISED; and producers of music videos and records who use similar labeling systems;
- encourages parents to responsibly monitor and control the viewing and listening habits of their children with popular media products (records, videos, TV programs, etc.);

Used with permission from NASSP. For more information concerning NASSP services and/or programs, please call (703) 860-0200.

- calls upon advertisers to take responsible steps to screen the programs they support on the basis of their violent and profane content;
- supports federal legislation designed to decrease and monitor TV violence including:
  a. H.R. 288, sponsored by Representative Edwin Markey (MA) and Jack Fields (TX), requiring TVs to be equipped with a V-chip, enabling viewers to completely block programs classified as violent by the networks;
  b. S. 942, sponsored by David Durenburger (MN), requiring the Federal Communications Commission (FCC) to develop and codify standards to reduce TV violence; and
- calls upon the Federal Communications Commission to initiate hearings on violence in the media, and to consider as part of those hearings the establishment of guidelines for broadcasters to follow during prime time and children's viewing hours; furthermore, the FCC should use its licensing powers to ensure broadcasters' compliance with guidelines on violence and establish a strict procedure to levy fines against those licensees who fail to comply.

National Association of Secondary School Principals Weapons in Schools Position Statement

WHEREAS   STUDENTS HAVE a right to attend school without a fear of weapons' violence to themselves or others;

Whereas   safe schools enhance the learning environment, necessary for quality schools, which are essential to a successful democracy;

Whereas   the causes for violence are multiple: chronic poverty, the lack of jobs and role models, the disintegration of families, the loss of moral values, and a popular culture that seems to glorify violence at every turn;

Whereas   a major 1993 Louis Harris poll about guns among American youth reports that 1 in 25 students have taken a handgun to school in a single month, and 59 percent know where to get a handgun if they need one;

Whereas   violence is exacerbated with the increase of weapons in our schools resulting in some 31 deaths from guns during the 1992–93 school year, be it therefore known that, The National Association of Secondary School Principals:

- supports passage of the Brady Bill which requires a waiting period and background check before legal purchase of a handgun;
- urges full enforcement of the Gun-Free School Zones Act of 1990;
- calls on Congress to pass the Safe Schools Act of 1993, with an amendment that will ban the purchase of a handgun and semi-automatic guns for any person under the age of 21;
- urges schools to provide staff training for weapons situations arising in school, and to implement student awareness programs which challenge youths' falsely held beliefs that they are invincible;

Used with permission from NASSP. For more information concerning NASSP services and/or programs, please call (703) 860-0200.

137

- challenges schools to implement apprehension, prevention, intervention, and counseling programs to combat possession of weapons and violent acts;
- encourages school-based parent involvement programs to include violence prevention strategies that emphasize the issue of easy access to handguns;
- exhorts school districts to establish violence prevention curriculum, grades K–12, and promote articulation among levels to ensure continuity in policies and practices;
- challenges Schools of Education to add conflict resolution and violence coping skills to their teacher preparation programs.

Teacher Discipline Style Inventory

Directions: Indicate how often you exhibit each of the behaviors when disciplining your students by placing a check in the column next to each statement according to the scale below.

Scale: A = Almost Never S = Sometimes F = Frequently V = Very Frequently

	Discipline Behavior	Frequency			
1.	I am unassertive in disciplining students.	A	S	F	V
2.	I tend to ignore discipline problems.	A	S	F	V
3.	I manipulate my students to motivate them.	A	S	F	V
4.	I exhibit great control over my students.	A	S	F	V
5.	I counsel my students on their misbehavior.	A	S	F	V
6.	I am indecisive in disciplining students.	A	S	F	V
7.	I tend to intimidate my students.	A	S	F	V
8.	I try to avoid disciplining my students.	A	S	F	V
9.	I can be "wishy-washy" with my students.	A	S	F	V
10.	I am personal, but assertive with my students.	A	S	F	V
11.	I am accommodating with my students.	A	S	F	V
12.	I tend to avoid discipline problems.	A	S	F	V
13.	I tend to be a dictator with my students.	A	S	F	V
14.	I tend to collaborate with my students.	A	S	F	V
15.	I tend to compromise with my students.	A	S	F	V
16.	I am a "soother/supporter" with my students.	A	S	F	V
17.	I tend to be apathetic in disciplining students.	A	S	F	V
18.	I am very assertive with my students.	A	S	F	V
19.	I am inconsistent in disciplining students.	A	S	F	V
20.	I take a "win-win" position with students.	A	S	F	V
21.	I "look the other way" with discipline problems.	A	S	F	V
22.	I am very sensitive about student's feelings.	A	S	F	V
23.	I aggressively take charge of discipline.	A	S	F	V
24.	I try to find "middle ground" with my students.	A	S	F	V
25.	I view discipline as a team approach.	A	S	F	V
26.	I try to be helpful and gracious with students.	A	S	F	V

139

27.	I send students to the disciplinary dean.	A	S	F	V
28.	I like to "give and take" with students.	A	S	F	V
29.	I can be threatening to my students.	A	S	F	V
30.	I talk with my students to reach a mutual result.	A	S	F	V

SCORING OF TEACHER DISCIPLINE STYLES SURVEY

Directions: Score each of the questions by giving a number for each question, using the point system below.

Very Frequently = 4 points;   Frequently = 3 points;
Sometimes = 2 points;   Almost Never = 1 point

Write the number of points for each question in the scoring line for each of the questions. For example, if you answered question number one with "Very Frequently," place a 4 on the line designated for question number one. If you answered "Frequently," give yourself 3 points. If you answered "Sometimes," give yourself 2 points, and if you answered the question "Almost Never," you would place 1 point on the designated line for question number one.

Place a point for each of the questions on the lines, respectively. When finished, add all the numbers for each column and put the total for each column on the line at the bottom.

	Supporter	Abdicator	Enforcer	Compromiser	Negotiator
1.	———				
2.		———			
3.				———	
4.			———		
5.					———
6.	———				
7.			———		
8.		———			
9.				———	
10.					———
11.	———				
12.		———			
13.			———		
14.					———
15.				———	
16.	———				
17.		———			
18.			———		
19.				———	
20.					———

21.		———		
22.	———			
23.			———	
24.				———
25.					———
26.	———			
27.	———			
28.			———	
29.			———	
30.					———
TOTAL	———	———	———	———	———

EXPLANATION OF TEACHER-STYLE SCORING

The interpretation of the Teacher Discipline Styles Inventory can be useful for examining your strengths and weaknesses in disciplining students. A high score for any given style indicates a preference for utilizing this style in disciplining students. A low score indicates that you do not have a preference in using this style.

If you scored high in the "Enforcer" category, it suggests that you use this style predominantly in disciplining students as compared to the other styles. If you are experiencing a great deal of disciplinary problems, it may be a result of utilizing this style too frequently. Excessive use of the "Enforcer" style may be creating more disciplinary problems since the students may resent the overuse of this style and rebel. If you had a low score in this category and you are experiencing frequent discipline problems, you might consider being more assertive in your disciplining of students.

If you scored high in the "Compromiser" category, it suggests that you tend to compromise frequently with your students. You may be viewed by students as being too inconsistent, "wishy-washy," and manipulative. The "Compromiser" style is also viewed as being too indecisive in dealing with students. A low score indicates that you do not compromise with your students.

If you scored high in the "Abdicator" category, it suggests that you tend to ignore disciplinary problems. The "Abdicator" is viewed as being reclusive and apathetic toward discipline problems. A low score may suggest that you have must confront every disciplinary incident, no matter how trivial they are. Use this style only for trivial disciplinary matters that need to be avoided.

If you scored high in the "Supporting" category, it suggests that you tend to overly accommodate your students when handling disciplinary problems. It also suggests that you may be overly mothering and protective of them. However, supporting a student may be the appropriate style to utilize when the student recognizes his/her problem and suggests a viable solution in resolving it. A low score in this category suggests that you do not have a preference in supporting your students.

If you scored high in the "Negotiator" category, it suggests that you handle discipline problems in a collaborative and mutual "win-win" approach with your students. The "Negotiator" style incorporates both an enforcing and supporting approach. This style is recommended as being the most effective style to utilize most of the time in disciplining students.

There may be times when any of these teacher discipline styles may be appropriate for a given disciplinary situation. For example, if a student is talking without permission, and the student recognizes this problem and states in a sincere manner to the teacher that he/she will improve, the teacher might support the student's position. In other cases, where a teacher must aggressively respond by enforcing a policy during a potentially life-threatening disciplinary situation, then the "enforcer" style may be appropriate. While you should strive to use the "negotiator" style most often, selecting the most appropriate style for a given disciplinary situation is the key to effective discipline.

Student Disciplinary Offenses Assessment

PROGRESSIVE DISCIPLINE SHOULD normally be followed when taking disciplinary action against a student. This process starts with counseling a student and continues through several stages leading up to expulsion. During each stage, mitigating circumstances should always be considered before rendering disciplinary action.

Directions: Please, individually, rate each of the student disciplinary offenses by placing the number that corresponds to the disciplinary action on the line adjacent to the offense. Please make the assumption that it is the student's first time offense. After you have completed your individual ranking, if you are working with in a group, rate each offense as a group.

Disciplinary Actions:

1. Counseling
2. Verbal Warning
3. Written Warning
4. Suspension
5. Expulsion

	Student Discipline Offence	Individual Assessment	Team Assessment
1.	Talking without permission	——	——
2.	Tardy to class	——	——
3.	Running in the hall	——	——
4.	Improper dress	——	——
5.	Defiance toward teacher	——	——
6.	Lying to teacher	——	——
7.	Smoking on school property	——	——
8.	Loitering	——	——
9.	Possession of tobacco products	——	——
10.	Using obscene gestures	——	——
11.	Writing profane language	——	——
12.	Leaving class without permission	——	——

13.	Indecent exposure	—— ——
14.	Extortion	—— ——
15.	Physical fighting	—— ——
16.	Assault	—— ——
17.	Battery	—— ——
18.	Theft of school property	—— ——
19.	Robbery	—— ——
20.	Arson	—— ——
21.	Bomb threat	—— ——
22.	Gang activity	—— ——
23.	Sexual violation	—— ——
24.	Use of intimidation	—— ——
25.	Drug usage	—— ——
26.	Possession of drugs	—— ——
27.	False fire alarm activation	—— ——
28.	Disruptive behavior on school bus	—— ——
29.	Persistent disobedience	—— ——
30.	Forgery	—— ——
31.	Possession of alcohol	—— ——
32.	Trespassing on school property	—— ——
33.	Absence without a valid excuse	—— ——
34.	Gross disobedience	—— ——
35.	Possession or use of pager or cellular telephones	—— ——
36.	Throwing objects in class	—— ——
37.	Rape	—— ——
38.	Sexual harassment of a student	—— ——
39.	Refusing to obey a teacher	—— ——
40.	Assaulting a teacher	—— ——
41.	Cheating on tests	—— ——
42.	Gum chewing	—— ——
43.	Smoking cigarettes in school	—— ——
44.	Stealing from teacher	—— ——
45.	Belittling another student	—— ——

Interpretation: Your individual and group ratings should be compared to those of your school or district. This instrument can also be used to develop a consensus for establishing a school- or district-wide uniform policy.

Teacher Class Management Survey

THE PURPOSE OF this survey is to assist you in identifying your strengths and weaknesses in class management.

Directions: Please evaluate yourself for each of the items by circling the number indicating the degree of frequency in exhibiting this behavior.

Frequency Scale:

1. Almost never
2. Sometimes
3. Frequently
4. Very Frequently

	Class Management Factors	Frequency Rating			
1.	I respect my students.	1	2	3	4
2.	I am consistent in administering discipline.	1	2	3	4
3.	I regularly motivate my students.	1	2	3	4
4.	I have concern and care for my students.	1	2	3	4
5.	I expect high performance from my students.	1	2	3	4
6.	I am committed to my students.	1	2	3	4
7.	I am objective and non-judgmental.	1	2	3	4
8.	I am sensitive and open with my students.	1	2	3	4
9.	I regularly praise my students.	1	2	3	4
10.	I try and improve the classroom layout.	1	2	3	4
11.	I am energetic with my students.	1	2	3	4
12.	I am calm and patient with my students.	1	2	3	4
13.	I am creative with students.	1	2	3	4
14.	I am cheerful with my students.	1	2	3	4
15.	I have an open mind with my students.	1	2	3	4
16.	I appreciate my students.	1	2	3	4
17.	I build the self-esteem of my students.	1	2	3	4
18.	I am enthusiastic around my students.	1	2	3	4

19.	I understand my school discipline policy.	1 2 3 4
20.	I explain my class rules to my students.	1 2 3 4

Total Score: —————————

Scoring: To determine your class management rating: Add your total score. A score of 70–80 = Excellent; 60–69 = Good; 50–59 = Fair; 49 & below = Needs Improvement.

Adams, J. (1965). Inequity in social exchange. In L. Berkowitz (ed.) *Advances in Experimental Social Psychology.* New York: Academic Press, 267–299.

Abernathy, S. et al. (1985). What stresses student teachers most? *Clearing House, 58,* 361–362.

Albert, L. (1989). *Cooperative discipline: How to manage your classroom and promote self-esteem.* Circle Pines, MN: American Guidance Service.

Albert, L. (1996). *A teacher's guide to cooperative discipline.* (rev. ed.). Circle Pines, MN: American Guidance Service.

Alderfer, C. (1969). An empirical test of a reference new theory of human needs. *Organizational Behavior and Human Performance, 4,* 142–175.

Angell, A. (1991). Democratic climates in elementary classrooms: A review of theory and research. *Theory and Research in Social Education, 19,* 241–266.

Augustine, D., Gruber, K., & Hanson, L. (1990). Cooperation works! *Educational Leadership, 47,* 4–7.

Banbury, M., & Herbert, C. (1992). Do you see what I mean? Body language in classroom interactions. *Teaching Exceptional Children, 24,* 24–28.

Bandura, A. (1977). *Social Learning Theory.* Englewood Cliffs, NJ: Prentice-Hall Inc.

Bartell, J. (1992) Starting from scratch. *Principal, 72,* 13–14.

Berne, E. (1964). *Games people play.* New York: Grove Press.

Blake, R. & Mouton, J. (1969). *Building a dynamic corporation through grid organization development.* Reading, MA: Addison-Wesley.

Blendinger, J., et al. (1993). *Win-win discipline.* Bloomington, IN: Phi Delta Kappa Educational Foundation.

Boothe, J., et al. (1993). The violence at your door. *Executive Educator, 15* (1), 16–22.

Brophy, J. (1987). Synthesis on strategies for motivating students to learn. *Educational Leadership, 45,* 40–48.

Brophy, J., & Putman, J. (1979). Classroom management in the elementary school. In D. L. Duke (Ed.), *Classroom management: The seventy-eighth yearbook*

147

of the National Society for the Study of Education (pp. 182–216). Chicago: University of Chicago Press.

Burke, K. (1992). *What to do with the kid who . . .: Developing cooperation, self-discipline, and responsibility in the classroom.* Palatine, IL: IRI/Skylight.

Cangelosi, J. (1997). *Classroom management strategies: Gaining and maintaining students' cooperation* (3rd ed.). White Plains, NY: Longman.

Canter, L. (1976). *Assertive discipline: A take charge approach for today's education.* Santa Monica, CA: Canter & Associates.

Canter, L. (1978). Be an assertive teacher. *Instructor, 88* (1), 60.

Canter, L. (1986). *Assertive discipline.* Santa Monica, CA: Canter & Associates.

Canter, L. (1988). Let the educator beware: A response to Curwin and Mendler. *Educational Leadership, 46* (2), 71–73.

Canter, L. (1989). *Assertive discipline for secondary school educators.* In-service video package and leader's manual. Santa Monica, CA: Canter & Associates.

Canter, L. (1992). *Assertive discipline: Positive behavior management for today's classroom* (2nd ed.). Santa Monica, CA: Canter & Associates.

Canter, L. (1993). *Succeeding with difficult students: New strategies for reaching your most challenging students.* Santa Monica, CA: Canter & Associates.

Cawthorne, B. (1981). *Instant success for classroom teachers, new and substitute teachers in grades K through 8.* Scottsdale, AZ: Greenfield.

Charles, C. (1996). *Building classroom discipline.* White Plains, NY: Longman.

Charles, C., & Senter, G. (1995). *Elementary classroom management* (2nd ed.). White Plains, NY: Longman.

Corno, L. (1992). Encouraging students to take responsibility for learning and performance. *Elementary School Journal, 93,* 69–83.

Curwin, R. (1980). Are your students addicted to praise? *Instructor, 90,* 61–62.

Curwin, R. (1984). High standards for effective discipline. *Educational Leadership, 41* (8), 75–76.

Curwin, R. (1988a). *Discipline with dignity.* Alexandria, VA: Association for Supervision and Curriculum Development.

Curwin, R. (1988b). Packaged discipline programs: Let the buyer beware. *Educational Leadership, 46* (2), 68–71.

Curwin, R. (1989). We repeat, let the buyer beware: A response to Canter. *Educational Leadership, 46* (6), 83.

Curwin, R. (1992). *Rediscovering hope: Our greatest teaching strategy.* Bloomington, IN: National Educational Service.

Curwin, R. (1993). The healing power of altruism. *Educational Leadership, 51* (3), 36–39.

Curwin, R., & Mendler, A. (1980). *The discipline book: A complete guide to school and classroom management.* Reston, CA: Reston Publishing.

Dewey, J. (1938). *Logic: The theory of inquiry.* New York: Holt, Rinehart & Winston.

Dobson, J. (1970). *Dare to discipline.* Wheaton, IL: Tyndale House Publishers.

Dobson, J. (1992). *The new dare to discipline.* Wheaton, IL: Tyndale House Publishers.

Dreikurs, R. (1968). *Psychology in the classroom* (2nd ed.). New York: Harper & Row.

Dreikurs, R., & Cassel, P. (1972). *Discipline without tears.* New York: Hawthorn.

Dreikurs, R., Grunwald, B., & Pepper, F. (1982). *Maintaining sanity in the classroom.* New York: Harper & Row.

Elam, S., Rose, L., & Gallup, A. (1996). The 28th annual Phi Delta Kappa/Gallup Poll of the public's attitudes toward the public schools. *Phi Delta Kappan, 96* (1), 41–59.

Emmer, E., Evertson, C., & Anderson, L. (1980). Effective classroom management at the beginning of the school year. *Elementary School Journal, 80,* 219–231.

Evertson, C. (1989a). Classroom organization and management. In M. Reynolds (Ed.), *Knowledge base for the beginning teacher.* Oxford: Pergamon Press.

Evertson, C. (1989b). Improving elementary classroom management: A school-based training program for beginning the year. *Journal of Educational Research, 83,* 82–90.

Evertson, C., Emmer, E., Clements, B., Sanford, J., & Worsham, M. (1989). *Classroom management for elementary teachers.* Englewood Cliffs, NJ: Prentice-Hall.

Evertson, C., & Harris, A. (1992). What we know about managing classrooms. *Educational Leadership, 49* (7), 74–78.

Firth, G. (1985). *Behavior management in the schools: A primer for parents.* New York: Charles C. Thomas.

Fraser, B., & O'Brien, P. (1985). Student and teacher perceptions of the environment of elementary school classrooms. *Elementary School Journal, 85* (5), 567–580.

Gallup, A., & Elam, S. (1988). The 20th annual Gallup poll of public's attitudes toward the public schools. *Phi Delta Kappan, 70,* 33–46.

Gaustad, J. (1992). *School discipline* (ERIC Digest No. 78) Eugene, OR: ERIC Clearing house on Educational Management.

Ginott, H. (1965). *Between parent and child.* New York: Avon.

Ginott, H. (1969). *Between parent and teenager.* New York: Macmillan.

Ginott, H. (1971). *Teacher and child.* New York: Macmillan.

Ginott, H. (1972). I am angry! I am appalled! I am furious! *Today's Education, 61,* 23–24.

Ginott, H. (1973). Driving children sane. *Today's Education, 62,* 20–25.

Glasser, W. (1965). *Reality therapy: A new approach to psychiatry.* New York: Harper & Row.

Glasser, W. (1969). *Schools without failure.* New York: Harper & Row.

Glasser, W. (1977). 10 steps to good discipline. *Today's Education, 66,* 60–63.

Glasser, W. (1978). Disorders in our schools: Causes and remedies. *Phi Delta Kappan, 59,* 331–333.

Glasser, W. (1985). *Control theory: A new explanation of how we control our lives.* New York: Perennial Library.

Glasser, W. (1986). *Control theory in the classroom.* New York: Harper & Row.

Glasser, W. (1990). *The quality school: Managing students without coercion.* New York: Harper & Row. (Reissued with additional material in 1992)

Glasser, W. (1992). The quality school curriculum. *Phi Delta Kappan, 73* (9), 690 – 694.

Glasser, W. (1993). *The quality school teacher.* New York: Harper Perennial.

Goldstein, S. (1995). *Understanding & managing children's classroom behavior.* New York: John Wiley & Sons.

Gordon, T. (1970). *Parent effectiveness training: A tested new way to raise responsible children.* New York: New American Library.

Gordon, T. (1974). *T.E.T.: Teacher effectiveness training.* David McKay.

Gordon, T. (1976). *P.E.T. in action.* New York: Bantam Books.

Gordon, T. (1989). *Discipline that works: Promoting self-discipline in children.* New York: Random Hose.

Grant, C., & Sleeter, C. (1989). *Turning on learning: Five approaches for multicultural teaching plans for race, class, gender, and disability.* Columbus, OH: Merrill.

Hakim, L. (1993). *Conflict resolution in the schools.* San Rafael, CA: Human Rights Resource Center.

Harmin, M. (1995). *Inspiring discipline.* West Haven, CT: NEA Professional Library.

Harris, T. (1967). *I'm O.K., You're O.K.* New York: Avon Books.

Hartzell, G., & Petrie, T. (1992). The principal and discipline: Working with school structures, teachers, and students. *Clearing House, 65* (6), 376–380.

Hernandez, H. (1989). *Multicultural education: A teacher's guide to content and process.* Columbus, OH: Merrill.

Herzberg, F. (1966). *Work and the nature of man.* Cleveland, OH: World Publishing Company.

Hill, D. (1990). Order in the classroom. *Teacher Magazine, 1* (7), 70–77.

Hughes, H. (1994, February). From fistfights to gunfights: Preparing teachers and administrators to cope with violence in school. Paper presented at the annual meeting of the American Association of Colleges for Teacher Education, Chicago.

Jones, F. (1979). The gentle art of classroom discipline. *National Elementary Principal, 58*, 26–32.

Jones, F. (1987). *Positive classroom discipline.* New York: McGraw-Hill.

Jones, J. (1993a). *Classroom management: Motivating and managing students.* Needham Heights, MA: Allyn & Bacon.

Jones, J. (1993b). *Instructor's guide: Positive classroom discipline—a video course of study.* Santa Cruz, CA: Fredric H. Jones & Associates.

Kameenui, E., & Darch, C. (1995). *Instructional classroom management.* White Plains, NY: Longman.

Kilmann, R. E., & Thomas, K. (1977). Developing a forced-choice measure for conflict handling behavior: The mode instrument. *Educational and Psychological Measurement, 37*, 309–325.

Knapp, M., Turnbull, B., & Shields, P. (1990). New directions for educating the children of poverty. *Educational Leadership, 48* (4), 1–8.

Kohn, A. (1993). *Punished by rewards: The trouble with gold stars, incentive plans, A's, praise, and other bribes.* Boston: Houghton Mifflin.

Kounin, J. (1977). *Discipline and group management in classrooms* (rev. ed.). New York: Holt, Rinehart & Winston.

Kramer, P. (1992). Fostering self-esteem can keep kids safe and sound. *PTA Today, 17* (6), 10–11.

Ladoucer, R., & Armstrong, J. (1983). Evaluation of a behavioral program for the improvement of grades among high school students. *Journal of Counseling Psychology, 30*, 100–103.

Landen, W. (1992). Violence and our schools: What can we do? *Updating School Board Policies, 23*, 1–5.

Macht, J. (1989). *Managing classroom behavior: An ecologica approach to academic and social learning.* White Plains, NY: Longman.

Mahoney, M., & Thoresen, C. (1972). Behavioral self-control—Power to the person. *Educational Researcher, 1*, 5–7.

Markoff, A. (1992). *Within reach: Academic achievement through parent–teacher communication.* Novato, CA: Academic Therapy Publications.

Maslow, A. (1943). A theory of motivation. *Psychological Review, 50*, 370–396.

McCormack, S. (1989). Response to Render, Padilla, and Krank: But practitioners say it works! *Educational Leadership, 46* (6), 77–79.

McGregor, D. (1960). *The human side of enterprise.* New York: McGraw-Hill Company.

McIntyre, T. (1989). *The behavior management handbook: Setting up effective behavior management systems.* Boston: Allyn & Bacon.

Mendler, A., & Curwin, R. (1983) *Taking charge in the classroom*. Reston, VA: Reston Publishing.

Morrison, J., Olivos, K., m Dominguez, G., Gomez, D., & Lena, D. (1993). The application of family systems approaches to school behavior problems on a school-level discipline board: An outcome study. *Elementary School Guidance and Counseling, 27* (4), 258–272.

Novelli, J. (1990). Design a classroom that works. *Instructor, 100* (1), 24–27.

Rardin, R. (1978, September). Classroom management made easy. *Virginia Journal of Education*, 14–17.

Redl, R. (1972). *When we deal with children*. New York: Free Press.

Redl, F., & Wattenberg, W. (1959). *Mental hygiene in teaching* (rev. ed.). New York: Harcourt, Brace & World.

Redl, F., & Wineman, D. (1952). *Controls from within*. Glencoe, IL: Free Press.

Render, G., Padilla, J., & Krank, H. (1989). What research really shows about assertive discipline. *Educational Leadership, 46* (6), 72–75.

Reutter, E. (1994). *The law of public education*, Westbury, NY: The Foundation Press, Inc.

Rich, J. (1992). Predicting and controlling school violence. *Contemporary Education, 64* (1), 35–39.

Rosen, L. (1992). *School discipline practices: A manual for school administrators*. Perrysburg, OH: School Justice Institute.

Schaps, E., & Solomon, D. (1990). Schools and classrooms as caring communities. *Educational Leadership, 48* (3), 38–42.

Schell, L., & Burden, P. (1992). *Countdown to the first day of school: a 60-day get-ready checklist for first-time teachers, teacher transfers, student teachers, teacher mentors, induction-program administrators, teacher educators* (NEA Checklist series). Washington, DC: National Education Association.

Schulman, J. (1989). Blue freeways: Traveling the alternate route with big-city teacher trainees. *Journal of Teacher Education, 40* (5), 2–8.

Schwartz, F. (1981). Supporting or subverting learning: Peer group patterns in four tracked schools. *Anthropology and Education Quarterly, 12* (2), 99–120.

Sharpley, C. (1985). Implicit rewards in the classroom. *Contemporary Educational Psychology, 10*, 349–368.

Sheviakov, G., & Redl, F. (1956). *Discipline for today's children*. Washington, DC: Association for Supervision and Curriculum Development.

Sidman, M. (1989). *Coercion and its fallout*. Boston: Authors Cooperative.

Skinner, B. F. (1948). *Walden two*. New York: Macmillan.

Skinner, B. F. (1953). *Science and human behavior*. New York: Macmillan.

Skinner, B. F. (1971). *Beyond freedom and dignity*. New York: Knopf.

Slavin, R. (1991). Synthesis of research on cooperative learning. *Educational Leadership, 48*, 71–82.

Slavin, R., Karweit, N., & Madden, N. (1989). *Effective programs for students at risk.* Needham Heights, MA: Allyn & Bacon.

Smith, M. (1993). Some school-based violence prevention strategies. *NASSP Bulletin, 77* (557), 70–75.

Sobol, T. (1990). Understanding diversity. *Educational Leadership, 48* (3), 27–30.

Sprick, R., & Sprick, M. (1993). *Foundations: Establishing positive discipline policies.* Longmont, CO: Sopris West.

Tauber, R. (1982). Negative reinforcement: A positive strategy in classroom management. *Clearing House, 56*, 64–67.

Tomal, A., & Tomal, D. (1994). Does your economic incentive system really improve quality? *Human Resource Development Quarterly, 5* (2), 185–190.

Tomal, D. (1992). Self management theory for developing teacher effectiveness: a new pedagogic approach to teacher effectiveness. *The Teacher Educator, 28* (2), 27–33.

Tomal, D. (1993). Staff development, filling gaps in teacher preparation. *The School Administrator, 50* (2), 51.

Tomal, D. (1997a). Collaborative intervention Process: A diagnostic approach for school improvement. *American Secondary Education, 30* (4), 17–24.

Tomal, D. (1997b, October). Discipline by negotiation: An alternative approach to managing discipline. Paper presented at the annual meeting of the Midwestern Educational Research Association, Chicago.

Vroom, V. (1964). *Work & motivation.* New York: Wiley.

Walker, H. (1979). *The acting out child: Coping with classroom discipline.* Boston: Allyn & Bacon.

Wattenberg, W. (1955). *The adolescent years.* New York: Harcourt Brace.

Wattenberg, W. (1967). *All men are created equal.* Detroit: Wayne State University Press.

Weade, R., & Evertson, C. (1988). The construction of lessons in effective and less effective classrooms. *Teaching and Teacher Education, 4* (3), 189–213.

Williams, S. (1991). We can work it out. *Teacher Magazine, 3* (2), 22–23.

Wolfgang, C., & Glickman, C. (1995). *Solving Discipline problems: Strategies for the classroom teacher.* Boston: Allyn & Bacon.

Wong, H., & Wong, R. (1991). *The first days of school: How to be an effective teacher.* Sunnyvale, CA: Harry K. Wong.

Zirkel, P. (1991). Corporal Punishment as a crime. *Principal, 71*, 62–63.

Zirpoli, T. (1995). *Understanding and affecting the behavior of young children.* Englewood Cliffs, NJ: Prentice-Hall.

155